# A
# COMMON PURPOSE

LIHÉ

# ENVIRONMENTAL EDUCATION AND THE
# SCHOOL CURRICULUM

WWF

These eleven essays have been commissioned by the World Wide Fund for Nature as one of a series of initiatives carried out by members of the Council for Environmental Education. They identify the position and purpose of environmental education within the school curriculum with particular regard to current debate concerning its structure and content.

Each of the essays represents a personal analysis of the contribution that each subject of the curriculum makes to a young person's total environmental education. It is hoped that they will provide insights and stimulate debate that will encourage those vested with the responsibility for designing and implementing the school curriculum to consider environmental elements as both a necessity and a benefit.

The choice of the cartoons of Leonardo de Vinci to illustrate this collection is significant. A feature of his genius was the desire to understand the subjects he painted as fully as possible. Thus the decisions he made as an artist were determined by insights into structure, form, function, cause and consequences that he gained from detailed investigation and experimentation.

Through education it is hoped that the professional and personal decisions that are made about the way we use the world's natural resources can be influenced by a similar level of insight.

Cover illustration: 'The Deluge' Leonardo de Vinci, courtesy of Her Majesty the Queen.

© 1988 Illustrations, Windsor Castle Library, Her Majesty the Queen.

© 1988 Text, WWF United Kingdom, unless otherwise stated.

ISBN  0 947613 06 4

FIRST EDITION 1988

Printed by Kingprint Ltd Richmond Surrey.

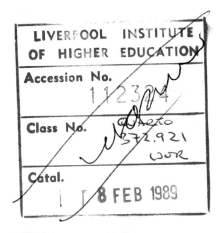

# Contents

# Introduction

Environmental education is fundamental to the future wellbeing of the planet and of its inhabitants. Through the exploration and development of insights, awareness, knowledge, skills and attitudes it develops essential competencies that enable people to make reasoned responses to the individual and social use of the environment.

Environmental education enables young people to understand, analyse and evaluate the relationship between people and their surroundings. This is achieved through: an understanding of the ecological processes that govern life on earth; an understanding of the geomorphic and climatic patterns that influence living things and human activity; an understanding of the social and cultural influences that determine human values, perceptions and behaviour; and an awareness of an individual's own personal relationship with the environment as a consumer, a producer and a sentient member of society.

These competencies are central to the quality of decisions, both intellectual and practical, that are made by individuals. They provide the potential for an informed use of the earth's resources with a full understanding of the consequences of actions. This is a prerequisite for a reduction in the damage to the environment, and subsequently society, by ill advised human activity and ultimately for an improvement in the quality of life for all people of the world.

Environmental education is not a subject in itself but a function of education with a content that is drawn from across the whole of the curriculum, and a pedagogy that espouses the notions of child centredness and active participation in the learning process.

Each subject area of the school curriculum focuses on, and explores, different aspects of human understanding and experience. Each subject can be mobilised to help young people develop their own coherent insight into human behaviour and the effect of this on people and the environment. Thus environmental education could be simply described as good education because it gives relevance to many different areas of the curriculum by providing a context to much of what is learnt. It gives breadth and balance by drawing on different views of our environment and encourages pupils to explore their own ideas and values, as well as being aware of, and tolerant to, the views of others.

The following essays explore the role of each subject in the development of such a coherent and relevant education.

# School grounds and the local area: their use as an educational resource

Photograph: WWF United Kingdom

Eileen Adams
Director
Learning Through Landscape Project

# School grounds and the local area: their use as an educational resource

## Experience

*"Nihil in intellectu quod non prius in sensu".*

All the interpretations of the concrete and abstract ideas which we derive from our encounters with our environment are the results in the first place of a myriad of sensory stimuli. Colin Ward[1] points to a continuous line of educational philosophers, from Plato through Rousseau, Schiller, Ruskin and Morris down to Herbert Read, who have all urged that education of the senses should be a central task of the teacher instead of a peripheral, marginal or optional extra:

*"the education of those senses upon which consciousness, and ultimately the intelligence and judgement of the human individual, are based."*[2]

Albert Einstein agreed that our perceptions of the external world are primarily dependent upon our physical (tactile) experience. Common speech, for instance, still equates 'tangible' with 'real'.

*"Out of the multitude of our sense experiences we take, mentally and arbitrarily, certain repeatedly occurring complexes of sense impressions (partly in conjunction with sense impressions which are interpreted as signs for sense experiences of others) and we attribute to them a meaning - the meaning of a bodily object."*[3]

This is further explained by E. H. Gombrich:

*"The world as we see it is a construct, slowly built up by everyone of us in years of experimentation. Our eyes merely undergo stimulations on the retina which result in so-called 'sensations of colour'. It is our mind that weaves these sensations into perceptions, the elements of our conscious picture of the world that is grounded on experience, on knowledge."*[4]

Hebb defines perception as the series of processes concerned with organising sensory stimuli from our environment for interpretation as the basis of understanding that environment and reacting to it. The function of perception is primarily to enable the individual to react effectively, whether that reaction is required immediately or stored for future use in the form of knowledge.

We operate within the limits of our previous experience and learning and we are capable of certain kinds of perceptions within those limits modified by our expectations, what is in our interest to perceive and what we want to perceive. This is open to further modification by subsequent experience and learning. Thus the individual's perceptual field is created early on, incorporating particular expectations and capacities, providing

> ## "The world as we see it is a construct, slowly built up by everyone of us in years of experimentation"

the basis for further cognitive and intellectual development.

Piaget's findings on intellectual development show that concept formation is directly related to a child's experience. This is the view of Frith, who sees the basic ability to conceptualise as being largely independent of language and mainly subject to experience. In fact he would go as far as saying that it is not the lack of language which is so detrimental to deaf children, but paucity of experience. This has implications for other children too.

The arguments for a rich experiential base for learning are already proven. For the teacher, the challenge is an awesome one - how to create significant experience for the child from which it is possible to develop capacities for thought, understanding and action; how to create experience as a rich magma of potential learning; how to exploit this experience as opportunities for learning; how to develop the ability to learn - to come to grips with new experience, unfamiliar ideas, new understandings, to make sense of them and derive meaning from them.

## Environment

In addressing the cross-curricular nature of environmental education, I assume consideration of the social and cultural environment as well as the physical environment, both natural and man-made. The school grounds and the local area can provide a wide range of environmental experience covering all these areas, both as a setting and as a subject for study.

For most children, the local area is likely to be an urban or suburban environment, providing a host of opportunities to explore complex relationships between people and place. Studies related to housing, work, the provision of goods and services, transport and communications, energy, resources, systems, social relations, cultural practices, government ... the list is endless. Convincing arguments for the use of the local areas were made by Colin Ward and Tony Fyson in the seminal book "Streetwork: The Exploding School" which enumerates the wide range of studies which can be undertaken through a range of subject specialisms.[5] These cover three broad areas of study:
*awareness* - how we perceive the environment; *systems* - how things work or evolve; *management* - how we shape and control the environment. These might be studies in relation to people, other

living forms, place, materials and resources.

## Local area

The challenge for both teachers and pupils is to look again at the ordinary, everyday and perhaps banal features of our lives in a familiar environment and invest them with new meaning and significance which has wider relevance for our lives. Developing awareness and understanding of the local area, its social and historical development, investigating how it came to be that way and questioning how it might be in the future, can provide an introduction to wider environmental issues and concerns. The use of the local area need not be parochial as long as the study is placed within a wider context - regional, national or international.

## School grounds

School grounds are growing in importance as an educational resource because of the greater emphasis in both primary and secondary schools on active learning and practical engagement. Costs and other problems associated with outside visits will increase and oblige schools to look afresh at the potential of their grounds as a resource for teaching and learning. However, perceiving the grounds anew is difficult for both teachers and pupils, who are likely to take them for granted and ignore them as a source of learning.

Much is known about children's need for richness and diversity of sensory experience, for varied encounters with the environment and the resulting stimulus and challenge this offers. School grounds provide an obvious and easily accessible environment for such learning to take place. They are a protected educational setting where an atmosphere and opportu-

nities to promote learning can be created. They can be seen as part of the continuum of learning experience inside and outside the classroom, a resource to extend educational opportunity through the extension of the learning environment into the 'sunshine classroom', the 'outdoor laboratory' or the 'pocket park.' A recent report by the Nature Conservancy Council [6] describes the ideal school grounds as
"*stimulating the imagination, promoting obsrvation and enquiry and integrating many strands of education.*"

> "School grounds are growing in importance as an educational resource because of the greater emphasis on active learning and practical engagement."

They can provide for both formal and informal learning, for pupils to be actively and practically involved: "*We need to use what is there, whether asphalt or grass. All sorts of skills can be learned, from digging to design*"[7]. These will necessarily be achieved through a variety of subject disciplines.

It is not the purpose of this paper to spell out the particular methodologies and understandings associated with each of the subjects in the proposals for the national curriculum and relate them to environmental education. Suffice it to say that each has its own concerns and its own framework for understanding, together with its particular methods of study which can all contribute to environmental education, but which necessarily give a partial and particular view when treated as discrete areas of knowledge. We might however discern certain sequences or patterns in the techniques employed which lead pupils through various activities, helping them to explore, observe, record, analyse, synthesise and communicate.

## Experiential learning

Although each subject discipline has its own unique framework and methodology for study, we may see general principles relating to all subjects engaged in environmental education. For instance, the use of the school grounds and the local areas as an educational resource relies heavily on the practice of experiential learning. This uses children's experience as its primary source material. Compared with desk-bound study, experiential learning requires a different kind of engagement with pupils, different relationships between teachers and pupils, between teachers and between the school and the community it serves. Previously, academic study and the use of texts and secondary source material has relied on the learning/teaching model of transmission - absorption - regurgitation, however attractively dressed up in kits and learning packages of various kinds. Here, although pupils might have engaged in exploratory or investigatory work, the implicit assumption on the part of both pupils and teachers has been that there is an outside authority, teacher or text book, that knows the answers and that the pupil's task is to seek out the received wisdom.

Experiential learning, however, is based on pupils' experience and builds on the basis of their knowledge rather than their ignorance. It requires a generative mode of learning and teaching, generating and sharing experience; reflecting upon and reworking that experience; deriving understanding and meaning from it; investing that understanding in further learning. The teacher's expertise here lies in learning methodology - what is being taught are the skills and methods of learning; what is being developed in the pupil is the capacity to learn and to apply the results of that learning.

This is particularly important in the case of environmental education, where we are subject to information overload in an area liable to constant change and development. It is inappropriate to promote environmmental education primarily through a knowledge-based curriculum. It is more important to develop the skills and capacities needed to confront the complex and dynamic area of experience and understanding. Malcolm Ross[8] characterises experiential learning as being distinguished by a commitment to the immediate and concrete, of experience with persons and things. It

> ## "The use of school grounds and the local area as an educational resource relies heavily on investigative study techniques."

has also been associated with a sense of involvement, challenge and achievement in terms of personal growth and self-realisation.

The use of school grounds and the local area as an educational resource relies heavily on investigative study techniques. It should be remembered that investigative learning is not confined to science subjects, but can be carried out through the medium of a range of subject disciplines. Different approaches mean that not all investigations have predictable outcomes. However, investigations should have a clear purpose, whether to encourage capacities for curiosity and exploration, or to develop observation and recording skills or to determine a course of action.

Pupils should understand not only the study methods involved, but the reasons for the investigation. There is a danger for instance, that the use of sampling techniques becomes an end in itself, whereas it should be understood as providing the basis for

analysis and evaluation. Similarly, experimentation need not be confined to the science laboratory, but can form part of art, design and social education.

A typical sequence for pupils, regardless of discipline, might be: environmental experience; observation; recording information; analysis; interpretation/reworking experience/connecting with previous learning; synthesis; communication of findings/understandings.

It is important that teachers identify appropriate learning methods in a variety of disciplines which develop a range of skills including: experiential, observational, discriminatory, recording, perceptual, conceptual, descriptive, analytical, interpretive, critical, expressive, communicatory. There are certain capacities which also need to be developed: the ability to question, to investigate, to identify, to classify, to order, to experiment, to develop and test hypotheses, to make inferences, to predict consequences, to handle and interpret data, to use reference material, to speculate, to imagine, to

hypothesise, to make choices, judgements, decisions, to describe, explain, qualify, evaluate, to quantify, to measure. To work in a concentrated, sustained and purposeful manner; to work cooperatively; to work independently. None of these are subject-specific, but can be developed through a variety of techniques from different disciplines and are a necessary part of engagement in environmental education.

### Fieldwork/streetwork

There may be tension evident in the difficulty pupils have in learning study techniques while at the same time attempting to use them effectively. There is a danger that pupils might employ certain methods without understanding their purpose. Other problems can impinge on the experience of working out of doors - the range and complexity of the stimulus; the need for focus and concentration; the difficulty in identifying what constitutes appropriate information and in selecting relevant

---

**On planning a study in the school grounds or the local area, teachers should take into account:**

| | |
|---|---|
| CONTEXT | what is the study derived from? |
| AIMS | what are the general educational aims? |
| OBJECTIVES | what are the specific learning objectives? |
| MOTIVATION | how to secure pupils' interest, engagement? |
| EXPERIENCE | what do they know already? |
| INTRODUCTION | stimulus, focus, starting point? |
| ENVIRONMENTAL EXPERIENCE | of what? |
| FIELDWORK | study methods (how to learn) |
| STREETWORK | teaching methods (encouragement, guidance, support, direction) |
| | organisation |
| | resources, equipment |
| | teacher input |
| CLASSWORK | anticipated problems/possible solutions |
| ANTICIPATED OUTCOMES | skills, capacities, knowledge |
| EVALUATION | what will be learned? how will you know? |

aspects; the need to work within constraints of time and weather; the possibility of disturbance and distraction. This raises the question of whether we need to adapt the environment to suit learning needs, as in the classroom or to adapt our learning methods to suit the particular environment in which we find ourselves and to exploit the opportunities for learning which it affords.

## Classwork

This paper has stressed the importance of direct experience as the basis for environmental education. However, we all know people who never seem to learn from experience. Experience in itself is insufficient. To learn from that experience we need to reflect upon it. It requires comparison with other experience, both direct and mediated to develop a fuller understanding of it.

Bruner[9] sees the function of language as a means of reordering experience.

"*Attention should be paid to the quality of childhood experience as a basis for intellectual development ... By encouraging a sufficiently rich experience and encouraging language development to order and understand that experience, we may contribute to improving the quality of life experienced by the child.*"

In the context of environmental education, we may regard the various subject disciplines as different 'languages'.

The ability to perceive and classify relationships is one aspect of language development, although classification can be carried out without the use of language. However, with increasing abstraction, it becomes essential. It is generally thought that the ability to classify is the basis of complex logical thinking. Cognitive development can be fostered by giving children as many pertinent experiences as possible, establishing learning conditions which will allow the child to see relevant dis-

tinctions in meaning and develop a differential classification of concepts. This is more effective when a number of subject disciplines is brought into play and these concepts are examined in familiar contexts.

## Environmental education in the curriculum

The proposals for the national curriculum identify maths, English and science as core subjects and a modern foreign language, technology, history, geography, art, music

> ## "If you accept an intolerable environment, you demonstrate an uncaring attitude to children."

and physical education as foundation subjects. There is a proposal that a number of 'themes' - environmental education is one of them -

"*should be taught through the foundation subjects, so that they can be accommodated within the curriculum but without crowding out the essential subjects.*"

This will satisfy those who see environmental education treated in a piecemeal and arbitrary manner in schools, dependent upon the interest of individual teachers and the imagination they bring to the interpretation of their subject syllabi. However, there is a need to provide for an explicit and coherent developmental pattern of multi-disciplinary study over a period of time, and in certain cases, provision needs to be made for inter-disciplinary study, in areas such as social education, ethics and environmental design. A parallel may be drawn with language development and English. Language is taught through all subject disciplines, but to be developed and refined requires the particular focus provided by English lessons.

There is the question of balance and bias in the various approaches; between quantitative and qualitative study; between subjective and objective methods; between group and individual working; between the collection and interpretation of data; between observation and reflection; between analysis and synthesis. It is necessary to examine each subject separately and in relation to others to consider the range of study methods actually used, the skills and capacities which they might develop, the ideas and understandings to be explored and the types of thinking to be promoted.

But it is not enough to think of environmental education in the school curriculum as an amalgam or conglomoration of studies pursued through individual subjects. Certain areas require inter-disciplinary study. One obvious area is that of environmental design. This is concerned with shaping, managing and controlling the environment and is centrally concerned with the notion of change. It is evident that participation in the design process changes pupils' perceptions of themselves, their environment and their capacity to accept change and the responsibility that goes with that. This will probably involve them in experience of decision making and the resolution of conflict, of issues of ownership and influence, all of which will be necessary to provide for full participation in a democratic society. The exploration of design issues related to the school grounds and the local area acts as a valuable introduction where pupils are encouraged to deal with change positively and creatively.

## School policy

This is all brought into sharp focus when a school attempts to devise a whole-school policy for environmental education and outdoor education. This brings into question the philosophy and practice of the various disciplines, the relationships between them,

6

curriculum content, the allocation of resources, support and organisation.

The formulation of such a policy is necessary to ensure some sense of coherence, progression and development in the pupils' learning experience. It is important that each successive engagement in environmental education should be more demanding and should widen experience or deepen understanding. This is particularly important when a number of disciplines share the same resource of the school grounds or the local area, when studies will not necessarily be seen as complementary, but could become repetitive.

When considering the potential of the school grounds or the local area as a resource, it is important to consider not only the environment itself, but teachers' perceptions too. In a recent study by the Learning through Landscapes Project,[7] enthusiasm, confidence and imagination were seen as important contributory factors in recognising the potential of such a resource and in conceiving ways of initiating and handling learning activities. Here, teachers' preparedness to be eclectic and opportunistic seemed particularly significant.

**Hidden curriculum**

In terms of influencing attitudes and values towards the environment, this study also revealed the importance of the hidden curriculum in environmental education: *"If .you accept an intolerable environment, you demonstrate an uncaring attitude to children. School grounds should be well kept, lively and attractive to children, colourful, friendly and welcoming. You want children to enjoy being at school and need to provide a creative environment with which they can interact. There is a need to establish the concept of the school environment as a real, changing environment rather than some dead, sterile place where children are* herded. *It should be an inspiration and offer a model for change, so that the attitudes and values children develop from their involvement with their environmnent will have a bearing on their lives later on."*

The hidden curriculum is also evident in the informal learning that goes on outside lesson time. The report goes on:
*"In terms of social learning through direct experience of others and through interactions with them, the school grounds, particularly the playground, is a learning environment of powerful significance. The nature of social relationships, behaviours and codes of conduct are all learned here through both positive and negative experiences. Experimentation with roles, experience of group membership, of differentiation of social groupings, of social control, are all learning experiences which children provide for themselves."*

Schools might be seen as communities in which pupils are citizens with the attendant rights, privileges and responsibilities that citizenship implies. It is important to give pupils the opportunity to acquire an understanding and appreciation of how their actions and decisions, now and later, affect the environment. It also reveals how a community develops its own accepted norms of behaviour and attitudes and how it exerts social control. All this is part of environmental education, but might not figure specifically in individual subject syllabi.

Similarly, developing care and responsibility for the environment may be stated in general aims, but might not find a place in specific learning objectives related to particular subjects. The affective domain and the fostering of caring attitudes towards the environment are significant aspects of environmental education, but are generally not learned through specific techniques, but through the ethos of the school. We cannot expect children to value that which is not evidently valued by the school. Often, respect and care develop through involvement and ownership. Effort should be made to provide pupils with environmental experience that creates the optimum conditions for such attitudes and feelings to develop. Thus an experiential base is important in the affective domain of environmental education.

Understanding the relationship between people and place is at the heart of all environmental education. The school grounds and the local area offer a very real focus for study, providing for emotional, social and physical experience of the environment, accessible and immediate for pupils.

© Eileen Adams, March 1988

**References**

1 Ward C. *'Can We Teach the Art of Seeing?'* Architectural Review, May 1978

2 Read H. *'Icon and Idea'* 1955

3 Einstein A. *'Out of My Later Years'* 1950 ref: Anthony Storr *'The dynamics of Creation'* 1972

4 Gombrich E.H. *'Art and Illusion'* 5th edition Phaidon Press Oxford 1977

5 Ward C. and Fycon T. *'Streetwork: The Exploding School'* 1973

6 Nature Conservancy Council Conservation Matters No 2 *'Using Primary School Nature Areas'* 1987

7 Learning Through Landscapes Research Project Working Paper No 1 1987

8 Ross M. *'The Aesthetic Impulse'* 1984

9 Bruner J. *'The Relevance of Education'* 1968

# Physical education

Photograph: Stuart Armstrong

Stuart Armstrong
Coordinator for Outdoor Education
Berkshire LEA

# Physical Education

## The philosophy

In the early years of childhood the need to develop physical skills is obvious and much time is devoted by parents to teaching their infants to walk, move and balance, for example. Similarly, where physical skills are lacking in an adolescent, the disadvantages, particularly in a social context, can be quite serious. As the young adult moves into the world of work, however, the need to be physically competent decreases for most of us. The need to be healthy does not. It is at this stage that the importance of

> ## "You don't realise how much you need it until you can't use it"

the skills and knowledge inculcated through Physical Education in the school years becomes so important. If a person has developed the habit of regular and appropriate physical exercise and a life style which is conducive to the preservation of health, then the teachers responsible have achieved all that could have been expected of them.

In reality, many adults, one is tempted to say most, do not retain the habit of keeping physically fit. What is worse, as many employers will tell you, is that many of us do not take steps to remain healthy at all and some become a burden on society for that very reason. As a nation we do not seem to regard physical recreation as the norm in adult life. How rarely do we hear of families saying as a matter of pride, or better still as if it were the most usual thing in the world, that they regard themselves as a sporting family? Rather, the reverse is more common. In our seemingly ever more utilitarian society, more efficient production and ever greater consumption seem to be the only valued goals.

Recreation becomes something one admits to rather shamefacedly. "*I just nipped off for a game of squash at lunchtime*" - as if one was being naughty rather than sensible. The important point is of course, rather as with the natural environment, we don't appreciate the value of what we have lost until it has gone. I would be a rich man if I had been given a hundred pounds every time I heard someone say, after injuring their back, "*You don't realise how much you need it until you can't use it*". In the same way health, fitness and a clean environment are all difficult to re-create.

But the link between physical well-being and the environment is not just analagous. To have a reasonable chance of staying healthy, one must live and work in an environment that is clean enough and natural enough to make this possible. How many times have I sat in a train coming out of London after a day of meetings and wondered what the experience has cost me in terms of my health? Apart from the tendency to eat convenience foods and rush stressfully about, the air can be positively unpleasant to breathe. How many times have I wondered also whether running alongside a road and breathing in carbon monoxide is doing me more harm than good and, in

the same moment, longed for the clean air of the hills? Translating this into implications for the Physical Education curriculum, it is apparent that an awareness of the importance of the environment in health and fitness is fundamental to an ability to make the most of one's physical potential in life. It is surely fundamental also if one is to enjoy physical activity. If you don't, what chance is there that you will make it a regular and frequent part of daily life?

## The role of outdoor education

It is in the field of Outdoor Education particularly, that the environment and physical skills come together as factors of equal importance. This unique situation has led to this becoming a field of concern and study in its own right but, as with any cross-curricular area, it merges imperceptibly with others at the margins. On the one hand the development of physical skills through, say, canoeing, sailing and hillwalking leads to very close links with Physical Education. On the other, an interest in, and concern for, the environment itself, an almost inevitable concomitant of involvement in outdoor pursuits, leads to close links with Environmental

---

**The identification and promotion of an environmental element in the broad church of Physical Education has additional benefits:**

it provides a challenge and purpose for P. E. outside the mere physical and thus can attract, involve and affect a broader array of young people than might otherwise be possible;

it could help to increase the scope, and therefore the credibility, of a subject which is often seen as having limited and very specialised value;

use of the environment for physical activity can cause damage - through erosion and disturbance, for example - and an environmental element in the curriculum could help to minimise this by encouraging more sympathetic use.

Education and fieldwork in Science and the Humanities.

For the individual, physical contact with the natural environment can present a wide range of inter-related personal challenges and interactions. These are experienced through physical, intellectual, emotional, aesthetic, spiritual and social components. Guided and structured experience of these components, even if experienced subliminally, can provide a broad based and enriching educational experience that can fundamentally affect the totality of a person's environmental education.

The links between Environmental Education and Physical Education exist then- and they are clear. It is the same environment for both and both have an interest in trying to ensure wise and sustainable use of it. For the same reason both are, or should be, concerned to develop an appropriate awareness and sensitivity in pupils, designed to lead in turn to positive action - what a Scottish Education Department document on Environmental Education referred to as "*the development of an attitude of stewardship*".

It would be counter-productive for these two arms of education to regard each other as being at war over the use of the common ground between them. Both areas are somewhere near the bottom of the subject hierarchy predicated in the National Curriculum. Both will probably have more limited curriculum time than previously. The drive for industry-like performance indicators of pupil attainment, whatever those indicators are to be used for, will use up enormous amounts of time in the core subjects. As ever, both will probably be expected to produce the same in less time - I have never yet seen or heard of a curriculum review that has recommended a reduction in the extent and depth of what pupils need to know. All this being the case the positive way forward is, surely, to identify areas of common interest, remove duplication and to advance the process of creating valid links in the minds of pupils between the physical and the environmental areas of knowledge. That way they will be better able to come to objective decisions

**"It is entirely possible to take pupils half way round the world and not to have achieved significantly more than could have been achieved in their home country."**

about their own health and fitness, and the quality of the environment they wish, or need, to live in.

If we are to develop this attitude of stewardship in pupils, then it must be done positively. A series of restrictive rules would not be helpful in achieving the objective. The environment would become yet another burden for young people to carry, rather than a thing of joy and a source of pleasure and absorbing interest. In just the same way as there are important habits to develop in any sport with regard to technique, there are surely positive habits to develop with regard to the ground being used. Such habits need to be based on an understanding of the logic and sense lying behind them and this is best taught as part of an integrated package. 'Bolt on' environmental awareness is a contradiction in terms.

## Implications for practice

I have referred to the National Curriculum in somewhat negative terms so far, but its very introduction could bring advantages in this area. Enforced change can provide an opportunity to break moulds and bring in new initiatives in a way that is difficult to arrange when there is no obvious need to

change in the first place. So, how could Outdoor Education be made viable in the 5% of curriculum time that it seems will be available to Physical Education?

Much can be done to introduce it on the school site, even within two periods. The first requirement is to look at the ground available through new eyes. Those corners beyond the touch line which the ground maintenance gang mower never reaches can provide ideal positions for orienteering markers. The area between the sports hall and the tennis courts, which is little more than a collecting point for odd bits of old equipment, could well be an excellent site for a climbing wall. Engineering its construction could present difficulties in both senses, but once there it should be a long lasting resource requiring little maintenance.

Exploring the area immediately around the school site, say within ten or fifteen minutes walking distance, can yield some gems as well. I recently visited a school with the name East Lake. As I am an Outdoor Educationalist, it seemed natural to ask where East Lake was and whether the school used it for outdoor work of any kind. It turned out that it did exist, was not used by the school and had been visited once by one member of staff by accident. Further investigation showed it to be ideal for introductory canoeing. What was more it was owned by the same local authority that owned and ran the school and the planning department had been wondering what they could use it for. A little way from paddling the white-water in the Grand Canyon, but nevertheless a very good starting point.

The process of finding, using and developing such areas can be enlightening for pupils in itself. More importantly, if done imaginatively, it can develop much more positive attitudes among

10

pupils to the potential and value of their own local environment.

More exotic locations are readily available today using short-stay residential facilities. There are essentially two problems with this approach. The first is time; specifically, staff time and curricular time. The second is money. Such approaches normally require substantial parental contributions and care has to be taken not to exclude those who might find it difficult to pay. I do not underestimate these difficulties, but I know of many schools where opportunities are made for such ventures. When well planned, they can lead to great benefits for learning in a wide range of subject areas. They can be invaluable as social experience and can contribute substantially to the ethos and positive traditions of an institution. They can also provide a useful target, topping out process, starting point or enhancement for courses based in school.

In this sort of exercise a thorough understanding of the aims and objectives involved and a very clear idea as to how they are to be achieved, is crucial. It is entirely possible to take pupils half way round the world and not to have achieved significantly more than could have been achieved in their home country. With this proviso, experience suggests that the only significantly limiting factor as to what can be done is the imagination and determination of the staff involved.

All these examples, and there are may others that could be cited, provide possibilities for schools to make more effective use of the environment in the teaching of Physical Education. In so doing, they provide the opportunity for pupils to develop sensitivity to, and appropriate concern for, the environment while at the same time learning to use it to best advantage for physical activity. It can greatly enhance what the Physical Educationalist can offer to pupils.It also facilitates the development of an attitude of stewardship to what is becoming ever more clearly a world of finite and dwindling resources.

©Stuart Armstrong, March 1988

### A final word

Physical Education, Outdoor Education and Environmental Education have one other important element in common. They all deal in the use of direct experience as a means of educatiing pupils. In a world in which much that children encounter is secondhand, often coming through the glimmering box in the corner of the room, this doing, this action based learning, is vitally important. Man is not a purely cerebral being. The ability to influence the quality of life and to interpret information and make objective decisions will stem in large part from accumulated experience. That direct experience of the outdoor environment which these areas of the curriculum can offer is capable of providing firm foundations on which a child's own developing experience can be confidently and reliably built. It is eminently sensible, as well as efficient, to consider how they can best work closely together to that end.

# The contribution of language teaching to environmental education within the national curriculum

Photograph: WWF United Kingdom

Elizabeth Baines
Freelance Educational Writer

# The contribution of language teaching to environmental education within the national curriculum

## Introduction

Young people throughout the world are becoming more and more concerned about environmental issues. There is a growing awareness amongst teachers too of the importance of environmental education for all pupils, but it may not be easy to see clearly how individual specialist subjects can contribute.

This paper aims to enable teachers of modern languages to appreciate the particular contribution that languages can make to environmental education, and to encourage the positive use of environmental materials in foreign language teaching.

There is of course no suggestion that, by deliberately including an element of environmental studies within its syllabus, any subject should lose its individual identity, or find that the content of its syllabus becomes unbalanced.

It may be of particular interest to language teachers to note that West Germany has recognised the interdisciplinary approach and the importance of environmental education in initial teacher training and in-service provision. As reported in the Times Educational Supplement of 23.1.87 in a statement from Frau Wilms, Education Minister:

*"The problem of reconciling economy and ecology, of integrating technology and culture, of protecting the interests of future generations must beome the object and objective of education."*

In France too, "L'Etude du Milieu' is also cross-curricular and is concerned with a 'sense of place', or an understanding of the 'milieu'.*

It is perhaps surprising that such a basic word as 'Umwelt' seems to be absent from GCSE German vocabulary lists, or 'environnement' or 'milieu' from French.

We are all part not only of a local and national community, but also of a global community. Our understanding of our involvement in this global community and our responsibility towards it are recognised as important aspects of environmental education. Such ideas are bound to be of considerable interest to language teachers and their pupils and could be developed further through some of the experiences gained in language learning.

By showing how environmental issues can play their own valuable part in language learning, it is hoped that some of the ideas expressed can be incorporated in foreign language syllabuses.

## Aims and objectives

Amongst the commonly stated aims of every language syllabus, three in particular seem to indicate a definite link with environmental matters. For example, aims included in a course leading up to the NEA examination in a foreign language are:

1 to offer insights into the culture and civilisation of other countries.
2 to encourage positive attitudes towards foreign language learning and to speakers of foreign languages and a sympathetic approach to other cultures and civilisations.
3 to provide enjoyment and intellectual stimulation.

One of the ways of achieving the human and social aims of foreign language learning is to make use of the flexibility of current GCSE

> "We are all part not only of a local and national community, but also of a global community."

syllabuses and choose stimulating materials which are both authentic and relevant. Of course, one of the inherent advantages of learning a foreign language is that knowledge of it can provide direct access to all manner of current issues in those countries in which it is spoken. One of the most fruitful areas of interest is that covered by environmental issues, which seem to be constantly in the news.

By reacting themselves to what they learn - both positively and negatively - pupils can be directed towards self-analysis, and encouraged to examine closely their own attitudes and opinions, especially where issues may be contentious. This could well be the case with such controversial matters as air and water pollution, disposal of nuclear waste, the damage to forests, hunting, or the threats to migratory birds.

If such issues are approached from original, 'foreign' angles, based on a range of authentic items presented in the foreign language, pupils will become increasingly aware of the international and global significance of environmental issues, since by their very nature their impact extends beyond national boundaries, implicating other countries and drawing attention to the consequences of their chosen environmental policies for other nations. They will find themselves having

---

* Mike Parry: 'Planning and implementing environmental curriculum initiatives in primary and secondary schools in England and Wales' (National Association For Environmental Education 1987)

to compare British attitudes with those of other countries involved and look critically at both sides of a given problem.

They will begin to appreciate how important it is for people - individually and collectively - to share a common interest and become involved in environmental issues. They will also see the need to encourage countries and their people to understand each other's attitudes and learn from each other's experiences, so that they can share responsibility and cooperate in order to find effective solutions to some of the problems raised.

Recent examples of issues affecting more than one country are the problems of air pollution and acid rain, the fire in Switzerland which caused poisonous chemicals to enter the Rhine, and of course the consequences of the Chernobyl accident.

Coming face to face in the original language version with the real attitudes and opinions of other people towards the environment can lead to a more valuable understanding of specific issues, rather than just relying on what is often an over-simplified or distorted English interpretation of a 'foreign' issue.

Pupils can gain different perspectives on the ways in which environmental issues can directly and indirectly affect people's lives and they can discover ways in which individuals of all ages and circumstances react towards them.

In Austria, for example, pupils in one school have organised a system for collecting waste paper which they then recycle, turn into stationery and sell back to pupils at cost. Another school has a highly efficient system for collecting organic waste for the compost heap in their organic garden. In Switzerland, a youth group organised a local campaign to persuade householders of the environmental benefits of spreading gravel, which the group delivered, rather than salt, to make their paths and drives safe in icy weather.

## Cross-curricular benefits

At this point it is perhaps worth emphasising the obvious cross-curricular benefits of including environmental elements in a foreign language course. Knowledge and experience gained in the foreign language may well provide an extra dimension to studies in other subjects. Real possibilities exist for a system of counter-credits whereby, for instance, evidence of a pupil's study in German of pollution of the Rhine could count towards an assessment unit in Geography, Chemistry or Commerce.

> "Pupils can gain different perspectives on the ways in which environmental issues can directly and indirectly affect people's lives "

Pupils may discover that they are particularly fascinated by a certain topic and wish to extend the knowledge gained in their foreign language learning into other school subject areas. A student of English may decide to make a special study of the significance of trees and woods to different people and consider the creative ways in which, through writing, drawing and music, for example, they express their feelings. An international dimension to such a study could prove extremely worthwhile.

Excellent materials exist which are specifically designed by various environmental organisations for the use of teachers in individual countries. Examples of these are: a German workbook produced in Switzerland on aluminium and recycling; a set of environmental work-cards produced in West Germany by a similar organisation to the Keep Britain Tidy Group; or a Swiss information action pack in French on six environmental issues in town.

Language teachers could join forces with colleagues in the same school or authority who teach in different disciplines to make use of such materials. This would enrich pupils' experiences in a wide range of subjects. Teaching colleagues may well open up links themselves to other foreign material through their own subject contacts and exchanges of teaching materials could take place.

## Resources

There are endless opportunities in language learning for making imaginative use of authentic materials based on current local and national environmental issues. These 'foreign' environmental resources are varied enough in appearance and content to appeal to all levels of ability, all ages and both sexes. A great attraction, which can provide extra motivation for pupils in schools, is that the written items are often originally intended for or produced by young people themselves, which can also make the language level more appropriate. Pupils may also begin to appreciate the relevance of acquiring language skills which can provide them with access to such areas of interest.

The format of such materials, especially those taken from young people's newsletters, magazines and posters, is inspirational and the presentation is often humorous. Amongst the items included are articles, readers' letters, poems and songs, surveys, diagrams and tabular information, cartoons, jokes, photos with captions, adverts, games, quizzes and competitions.

A regular and changing supply of fresh materials can have a positive effect on pupils' motivation. It can also boost confidence when they recognise that they are often able to read about new issues in the language of the country concerned and discuss them before they become common knowledge in Britain.

As an illustration of the range of items, the September 1987 German edition of World Wildlife Fund Switzerland's Panda Club magazine for young people contains a strip cartoon based on the 'green' character, Gabi Grün, and information about CFC aerosol spray cans. The main article is about soil and organic farming, with a suggestion to readers to write to a local organic farmer and send a drawing of their ideal farm. Other editions contain a completely different collection of items.

## Treatment

The treatment of environmental topics will naturally vary according to pupils' abilities and the level of their linguistic experience. There is an opportunity to encourage pupils to widen their areas of interest and break out of the traditional mould of 'interests and hobbies' based on sport and entertainment. Many of the topics lend themselves to a group or pair work approach.

For example, after an initial introduction via photos and cartoon to the theme of waste, pupils could divide themselves into a range of 'recycling' groups on glass, paper, aluminium, batteries and organic waste. They could then analyse a selection of information from various 'foreign' sources, consider some of the ideas put forward, test some of them out and present their findings to the rest of their class in any way that seems appropriate. These presentations could perhaps take the form of a survey or questionnaire, or rely on information presented visually.

## Audio and visual materials

The emphasis so far has been placed on the possible range of materials produced in a written form, which can be used as a stimulus for oral and written work, as well as to encourage wide and purposeful reading. Various environmental organisations abroad do produce selections of slides, cassettes, videos and films aimed at young people which can be linked in with the topics which pupils have already read about and discussed. They are also in a position

> "The inclusion of materials from countries which are often less familiar to British pupils learning a foreign language can enrich pupils' experience and help to break the longstanding stranglehold of items from France, West Germany and Spain over authentic sources."

to recommend relevant radio and television programmes for recording, which could perhaps be exchanged between linked classes, as is of course the case with other 'interest' topics selected for language study. "Environmental" themes frequently crop up in both BBC and ITV language broadcasts for schools and adults, and they also feature in commercial language courses for schools.

## Diversification

Whatever the language - and it is acknowledged that we must diversify the choice of languages available in schools - materials are readily available from various environmental organisations, including the individual WWF national organisations in Europe and beyond.

The inclusion of materials from countries which are often less familiar to British pupils learning a foreign language can enrich pupils' experience and help to break the longstanding stranglehold of items from France, West Germany and Spain over authentic sources.

In Austria and Switzerland, for instance, there are many committed and articulate young environmentalists, and various environmental organisations are only too willing to provide them with a forum for debate through their own attractively produced magazines, newsletters, posters or leaflets.

Examples from the French edition of the Swiss magazine Panda Club include "Poisson Rallye' - a game based on the adventures of a small fish on its journey from stream to river to sea, a series on 'L'Arbre' with photos linked to children's creative writing about trees, and an article about mopeds and their component parts from the third world.

German examples include a regular series on the idea of the month, ranging from how to watch birds from your sick bed to testing snow for pollution, a series on recycling and articles about greening the city.

Organisations in South America, Africa, Belgium, and Canada also produce a variety of environmental items. Countries as small as Martinique may prove to be an interesting source of contrasting materials.

For example, in one publication by the Ministry for the Protection of Nature in Senegal, there are photos of posters on saving water and recycling rubbish, a cartoon on noise pollution and short articles on air and noise pollution and the problems of refuse disposal.

## International contacts

If, on a regular basis during their foreign language learning, young people in Britain come to enjoy studying and discussing other young people's reactions to and experiences of real, live environmental issues in other countries, then they may be motivated to pursue their interest by forming class links or individual links with young people abroad. These links can go beyond the usual exchanges of information based on hobbies and family and go some way towards satisfying a healthy curiosity about bigger issues too.

Such links can present pupils in a range of different countries with an ideal opportunity to exchange ideas, to ask questions, to compare experiences and attitudes, and to test and analyse each other's opinions.

The form in which these exchanges takes place can of course vary: pupils may wish to exchange tapes, compile questionnaires and design visual materials such as cartoons or leaflets, as well as write letters and messages and exchange relevant newspaper and magazine articles. They can decide which language to use, consider different ways of helping their partners learn a foreign language, and gain a genuine and lasting impression of how young people in another country feel about real issues.

Mutual experiences of this kind may genuinely lead to a greater international understanding and foster an awareness and sensitivity to differences in attitudes between nations. A foreign country, its language and people can become more of a reality. School links and pupil-to-pupil exchanges may arise as natural consequences of encouraging such enjoyable communication between young people from different countries.

**Beyond the classroom**

As a result of becoming more familiar with environmental issues, pupils may be keen to do something positive themselves to improve their environment locally. They may feel encouraged to extend their desire for environmental action not only into the immediate environment of their own school but out into the community, involving family, friends and neighbours.

Made confident by their knowledge of what has proved to be successful in other countries, their ideas for practical conservation may range from creating a small pond or butterfly garden to organising school or community-based recycling initiatives.

© Elizabeth Baines, March 1988

### Conclusions

1) The need exists both to raise environmental awareness generally and to satisfy the interest shown by young people in current environmental issues.

2) The imaginative use of environmental materials from various countries would broaden the linguistic experience of foreign language learners.

3) The motivation gained from the forging of individual or class links between pupils with a common interest in the environment can help to develop both social and communication skills.

4) Where environmental topics provide an opportunity for cross-connection between language learning and learning in other subjects, then pupils should be given the appropriate additional credit.

5) Environmental knowledge gained in the classroom can be translated into practical environmental benefit around the school and out in the community.

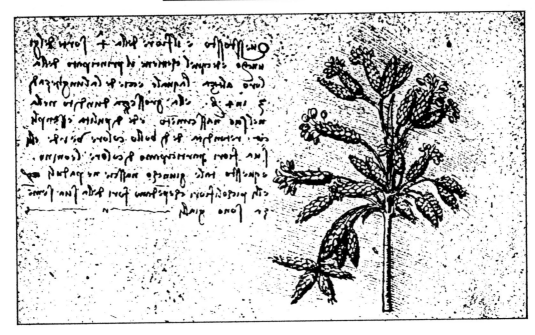

# Mathematics and environmental education

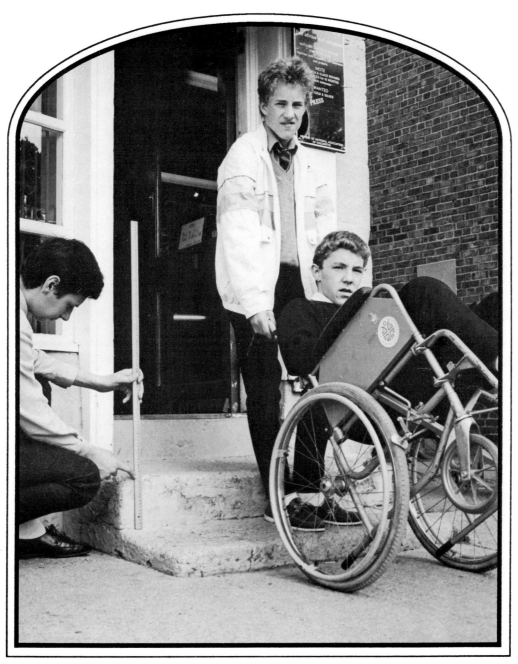

Photograph: WWF United Kingdom

Nigel Bufton
Head of Mathematics
Mathematics Centre West Sussex Institute of Higher Education

# Mathematics and environmental education

In 1919 a report by the Mathematical Association on the Teaching of Mathematics in Public and Secondary Schools recommended that a:

"*mathematical education should enable pupils not only to apply mathematics to practical affairs, but also to have some appreciation of those greater problems of the world, the solution of which depends on mathematics and science*".

Nearly seventy years later, in the light of the introduction of a proposed National Curriculum, we might ask whether this should remain a valid aim, and if so, how might we ensure we achieve it?

For many people their recollection of their own classroom mathematics is of a dry and routine affair littered with meaningless symbols and unintelligible rules. Occasional relief would be provided to make models, collect unused data or even play with games and solve puzzles, but these would soon be replaced by the 'proper mathematics' of usual routine exercises. There would be little or no experience of using mathematics to gain an insight into human behaviour or an understanding of the world in which we live. As a consequence of this, there has developed a view of mathematics as a dull, hard, theoretical activity, beyond the comprehension of the 'average' citizen and useless but as a provider of those basic skills needed in everyday living.

The National Curriculum must not legitimise this outdated and inaccurate view. For mathematics is a rich, vibrant and accessible activity with innumerable applications and uses; the National Curriculum could provide the opportunity for recognising and supporting this by ensuring that richness and accessibility can flourish and by offering pupils a diverse approach to learning which includes cross-curricular application. However, by imposing on our schools attainment targets, and programmes of study which will "*set out the overall content, knowledge, skills and processes relevant to today's needs which pupils should be taught in order to achieve them*", (para. 26, National Curriculum 5 - 16), there is a danger that this could be treated as a return to

> "mathematical education should enable pupils not only to apply mathematics to practical affairs, but also to have some appreciation of those greater problems of the world, the solution of which depends on mathematics and science"

those narrow utilitarian values. It could lead to a restricting of pupils' curriculum experiences.

Much of the conventional mathematics content found within the school syllabus today arose through application, through a need to find solutions to "problems of the world". These past problems may no longer be of pressing concern in our current lives but problems still exist and mathematics has its part to play in their resolving. Why, then, should we seek to impart the content without providing some of those problems that reflect the spirit within which this mathematics first arose? The environment in which we live is a ready provider of problems. It is a resource for the delivery of the content. As we use mathematics to help clarify our understanding of the world we inhabit, so too do we gain insight into the structure of the subject. Concentration on routine skills, devoid of any meaningful context, offers no opportunity for the young person being educated either to make judgements about the appropriateness of the subject area to other issues or to use mathematics to affect decisions and observe their consequences. Skills and strategies like these are essential requirements for taking an active role in today's world.

We owe it to future generations to ensure that they understand and can begin to tackle many of the problems they will inherit, as well as just deriving any of the resulting benefits. The aim quoted above is still valid. Young people can appreciate those "greater problems of the world" as they explore mathematics. For mathematical experience is enlivened by study through application, but it will be stifled by a return to utility. Pupils can extend their understanding and knowledge and at the same time develop those personal qualities of:

"*self-reliance, self-discipline, and enterprising approach and the ability to solve practical real-world problems, which will stand them in good stead in later life*", (para 68, National Curriculum 5 - 16).

These are not exclusive activities; they do not require additional and discrete courses on life skills, enterprise, problem solving etc. Much depends on the attitudes and approaches taken to teaching and learning. It is necessary that within the subject area there are clear aims which relate to these processes and which support, and are supported by, the experience offered to pupils. If mathematics is treated as an active process in which the learner is expected to take his or her share in the responsibility of acquiring skills, knowledge and understanding, then these aims are in operation. Such participation will require the teacher and learner to be involved in negotiation, discussion, the use of judgement, decision making, team work and other skills valued by society and in the world of work. It is a move away from the model in which the pupil is a passive receiver of knowledge, formally tested by external bodies on content alone. Active learning requires active assessment. It must recognise that pupils will acquire disparate forms of knowledge, a consequence of the enterprise, self-reliance and self-discipline nurtured in the learner.

> "To gain an insight into our environment pupils must become intelligent observers aware of their own view-points as well as those of others."

The National Curriculum Mathematics Working Group is charged with the task of ensuring that the programmes of study they produce foster those personal qualities quoted above and set out to equip every pupil with the "*knowledge, skills, understanding and aptitudes to meet the responsibilities of adult life and employment.*" (Terms of Reference). Consideration is also to be given to various cross-curricular themes of which "environmental education" is one. The task is a major one. It requires careful consideration as to the practical logistics for the classroom. The stated aims and objectives must be realisable and the programmes of study sufficiently broad and flexible for pupils to follow such themes when asked to do so, unhindered by content restraints. There must be present an emphasis on the need to develop in pupils a spirit of enquiry, to provide opportunity for pupils to explore, to ask questions, to conjecture, to provide evidence, to formulate argument, to convince, to prove.

To gain an insight into our environment, pupils must become intelligent observers, aware of

their own view-points as well as those of others. They require skills to help them make qualitative and quantitative judgements. Through mathematics such skills can be engendered. Pupils can be given problems to solve that relate to the environment, which contain some practical emphasis, which provide some in-depth study, and which may require a deterministic or stochastic model of a simulation exercise. Indeed, if pupils are to be made more environmentally aware through mathematics, they must spend time in that environment, outside the classroom confines, faced with tasks that necessitate making contact with people, with the world of work or with other aspects encountered in our every-day living. These tasks require preparatory discussion and careful planning, but should promote initiative and the making of informed judgements. There must be opportunity for pupils to decide what quantitative attributes are important, what to measure, how to measure, how to display, how to interpret, how to code, how to analyse, how to generalise, how to predict, how to evaluate.

Using mathematics to arrive at, and to support, decisions taken, does not in itself mean that those decisions were the correct ones. Mathematics is often insensitive to the realism of the solution obtained. The user of mathematics made the initial assumptions which led to the solution. It is his or her responsibility to test the authenticity of the results in the light of the assumptions made. The kind of environmental tasks pupils undertake might have some inbuilt checking mechanism and pupils should be encouraged not to see their solution as the end point. The full ramifications of their decisions may be broad and too far reaching, but where possible assessment should recognise any considerations of the solution's practicability.

In mathematics teaching such activity has been gathering pace, firmly supported by those aims

stated in the National Criteria for GCSE (1985). GCSE mathematics courses should now enable pupils to:
"*develop an understanding of the part which mathematics plays in the world around them*" (aim 2.4), "*solve problems; present the solutions clearly, check and interpret the results*" (aim 2.5) and "*recognise when and how a situation may be represented mathematically*" (aim 2.7). Coursework is intended to provide an opportunity for pupils to conduct co-operative and extended enquiry.

Many ideas for such enquiry can be taken directly from local or national news items. Recently, for example, the hurricane that struck the British Isles felled millions of trees and wreaked millions of pounds worth of damage. We were given estimates for the respective millions. Pupils might be asked to consider what 15 million damaged

> "GCSE mathematics courses should now enable pupils to 'develop an understanding of the part which mathematics plays in the world around them'"

trees look like, to think about how much space they take up and how the estimates were made. What volume of wood was involved? How to find the volume of wood for one tree. Is the trunk uniformly circular? How to find the area of a circle from the circumferences to produce a formula table or graph to give area from circumference. How many circles should we measure? How to find the height of a tree and the lengths of branches. How to estimate its monetary worth. What proportion of the British Isles is covered by trees? How to find the area of those irregular green shapes on the map. How to scale up. How to estimate the number of trees per hectare.

How to find their value. What is the cost of 15 million trees? Such news items offer many ideas for pupil enquiry and many questions for pupils to try to answer.

Nowadays, attention is often drawn to the quality of life, the standard of living and the care of the sick. Judgements about these issues are made from collected data but different interpretations are often given to the same statistics. How, for example, might our

> "It is not just that 'environmental education' can be included within mathematics but that it should."

pupils view the quality of their lives? What measures would they choose to use? How might they consider measuring them? How to present them, how to interpret them, how to make informed judgements; should they generalise these? Are these judgements less valid than those of the newspaper pundits? Statistical averages offer representatives and summaries, the techniques enable some hypotheses to be tested and any association between variables to be identified as likely contributors. The statistical syllabus is intended for such analysis and society's concern about the human condition is often judged through some quantitative measure. The smoker is informed that cigarettes damage health but continues to smoke. How many pupils in an 'average' school smoke and how aware are they of the likelihood of suffering lung and other damage? What is the chance their health will be affected? How early do they start smoking? How much are they likely to spend on tobacco? Can a school influence the attitude of its pupils in matters of health care? Surveys and questionnaires require careful attention to their construction, and detailed thought about the randomness/stratifica-

tion of samples and their representation of the underlying population.

School rules about no dropping of litter reflect our desire to keep our environment clean. Yet at the same time containers and packages are designed simply to be discarded. The managers of our resources give attention to the cost of recycling and the cost of total discard. However, many containers are designed simply to display and protect the goods they enclose, and it does not make economical sense for them to be recycled. Pupils can be asked to design containers of their own to hold a variety of different items. What criteria should be used to judge a 'good' container? Does it look attractive? Will it stack sensibly? Is it easy to use? Is it strong enough? How much stronger is card than paper? Can it be re-used? Is it cost effective? How much less card is needed to reduce volume by 10%? What shape uses the least card? Can a general expression be derived for the volume and/or area? Practical geometry is needed in the construction; algebraic skills are brought to the general formula. Calculators and microcomputers facilitate further exploration. These activities also offer an assessment of the end product in the light of those real considerations determined by the criteria. The pupils awareness of space and the rules governing geometrical structure are enhanced.

The space in which we live needs management. Those buildings old and new in our environment offer opportunity for further work in geometry, town planning, provision of amenity areas, design of schools, activity relating to number and measure, area, volume, and data collection, use of buildings, who lives where. The change in our environment offers opportunity for prediction. Populations rise and fall. Can they be predicted? Roads, houses and shops are demolished and built. Hills are flattened, the earth is moved. How to find the volume of

earth in an embankment, the bricks and wood in a house and the food held in store in a shop. What food contains grain? How much grain do we eat? How much land do we need to grow it? If one acre is cultivated in wheat, how much will it yield? How many people will it feed? For how long? Is the total yield predictable? What variables should be taken into account? Can the yield be determined by a formula or should there be an element of chance built in to account for fluctuations in the weather? How do we model weather? What is a typical year's weather and how much does it vary?

Our own bodies also provide a mathematical resource. We are governed by cycles. We oscillate between waking and sleep. Our heart beats regularly and our temperature varies periodically. The sinusoidal wave form offers an analogy; the tides of seas and rivers, the swing of a pendulum and the motions of the planets present further cycles for exemplification and analysis.

There is ample opportunity too to engage in cross-curricular work initiated by the activities. Through scientific experimentation and analysis, construction and craft design technology, historical data collection and interpretation and the diversity of approaches followed by pupils, there can be shared teaching and a common pursuit of aims. It is not just that 'environmental education' can be included within mathematics but that it should. The experiences of pupils will be the richer because of it.

©Nigel Bufton, March 1988

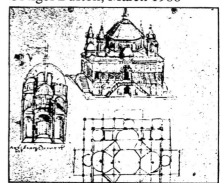

# Environmental education in the science curriculum

Photograph: WWF United Kingdom

Andrew Hunt
Project Director of the SATIS 16-19 Project
of the Association for Science Education

# Environmental education in the science curriculum

Some see the advent of a National Curriculum as a threat; others regard it as a challenge. The purpose of this paper is to show that in the new context there are plenty of opportunities to build on existing good practice in secondary schools so that by the end of the compulsory education more young people have an enhanced understanding of the world around them and the confidence to take part in the debate about environmental issues.

The Science Working Group for the National Curriculum is developing its proposals within the framework of the DES Policy Statement *Science 5–16*.[1] This statement includes ten principles for the analysis of science programmes including the following which are the sub-headings in this paper: breadth and balance, relevance, teaching methods, continuity and progression.

> "The move to balanced science has required a reappraisal of the way in which science programmes are organised"

Following the introduction of GCSE, the move to 'balanced science for all' is now one of the main preoccupations of secondary-school science teachers. At the same time there are demands for the introduction of a number of cross-curricular themes, and so the call for a coherent strategy for environmental education has to compete, among other things, with demands for the implementation of IT, health education and technology across the curriculum. Faced with many pressures, science teachers are more likely to respond to down-to-earth, practicable proposals rather than generalised exhortation.

In 1980 the World Conservation Strategy presented a powerful case for sustainable development linked to the maintenance of the Earth's life support systems and the preservation of genetic diversity.[2] Grand statements of this kind can provide a rationale for environmental education, but they seem very remote from the perspective of a typical secondary school science laboratory.

How can we ensure that science courses in future help young people to understand environmental problems, give them the opportunity to acquire technical skills, and encourage them to develop a feeling of involvement and capability, so that, as citizens in a democratic society, they will seek to promote the cause of environmental protection?

## Breadth and balance

The move to 'balanced science for all' has required a reappraisal of the way in which science programmes are organised. Many courses in future are likely to be either integrated or co-ordinated and lead to a double certificate at GCSE. The two examples discussed in this section show that both models can provide for a strong component of environmental education.

### NEA Modular Science[3]
This integrated-science syllabus has proved to be very popular, so that it has been widely adopted and not just in the North of England. For a double-award the students must study four core modules and ten option modules chosen from twenty two.

One of the core modules is called *The Environment*. The syllabus is based on five questions:
◊ Why do different plants grow in different places?
◊ How do plants and animals in a habitat affect each other?
◊ How do plants get their food?

◊ How does the environment keep going?
◊ Why is there such concern about the environment?

While seeking answers to these questions, students are expected to develop and apply their knowledge and understanding of plant nutrition, soil, habitats, food chains and webs, populations, energy transfers, natural cycles as well as the interaction of human activities and the environment. A wide range of learning experiences is suggested including the collection and analysis of data, practical investigations involving measurement and the control of variables, computer simulations, as well as discussion and debate. The list of suggested experiences mentions field work as well as laboratory experiments; it also suggests that students should research and evaluate the success of campaigns to protect endangered species.

Opportunities for environmental education in this syllabus are not limited to the core module. There is an option module about *Earth Science* and three other modules called
*Managing resources*:
1. *Water*
2. *Food*
3. *Waste and pollution*

The *Food* module is particularly interesting because it touches on two of the key points in the World Conservation Strategy: the preservation of soil as a key life-support system and the need for conservation to maintain genetic diversity.

This syllabus makes clear that introducing environmental topics can put science in context and thus show students the relevance of what they are learning to the everyday things with which they are familiar. Environmental contexts thus serve the needs of science education by providing opportunities for the deployment of practical and intellectual skills.

## Nuffield Co-ordinated Sciences [4]

This new scheme is attracting a great deal of attention because it allows schools to move to balanced science while retaining the identity of the separate sciences.

The strategy for co-ordination is explained in the Teachers' Guide and is based on the principles which connect Biology, Chemistry and Physics. The approach is illustrated by three charts showing the inter-relationships for energy, particles and the environment. The environment chart is reproduced below; it makes clear that environmental education is not limited to Biology, but can also be used to provide contexts for the physical sciences.

The GCSE syllabus for Nuffield Co-ordinated Sciences [5] has been developed in accordance with the new National Criteria for *The Sciences: Double Award.* Thus it includes these aims:

1.1 to enable pupils to acquire understanding and knowledge ... so that they may become confident citizens in a technological world, able to take or develop an informed interest in matters of scientific import.

3.2 to stimulate interest in, and care for, the environment.

4.2 to promote awareness that the application of sciences may be both beneficial and detrimental to the individual, the community and the environment.

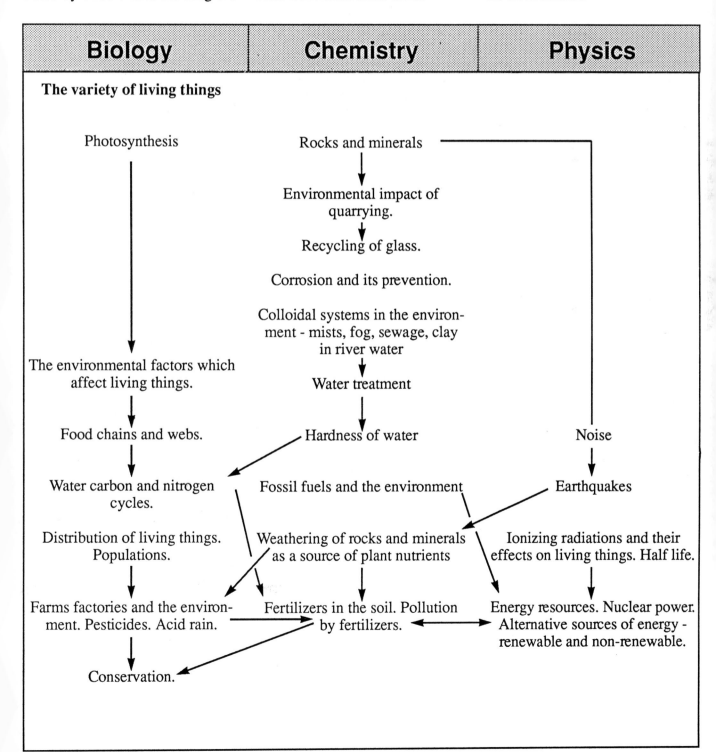

NCCT. Nuffield Co-ordinated Sciences *Teachers' Guide.* Longman, 1988

The assessment objectives state that pupils will, among other things, be expected to:

1.5 show knowledge and understanding of everyday and technological applications with their personal, social, economic and environmental implications;

2.6 explain everyday and technological applications of science and evaluate associated personal, social, economic and environmental implications.

## Relevance

The DES Policy Statement says that science education should draw extensively on the everyday experience of pupils and should be aimed at preparing them for adult and working life.

The importance of 'relevance' is explored in the third of the Curriculum Guides published by the Secondary Science Curriculum Review [6] The Guide suggests three ways in which science can be applied by pupils:

◊ as they learn to investigate phenomena and seek to understand the world;

◊ as they attempt to solve practical or technological problems;

◊ as they endeavour to formulate views on some of the science-related social and ethical issues that confront them as members of contemporary society.

The Guide puts forward strong arguments for putting school science in context; among five suggested contexts it proposes that pupils should study science in relation to the natural world and the interactions of science and technology with the environment (local, national and global).

In response to the call for 'relevance' the Association for Science Education sponsored the SATIS project which has published a bank of 100 short units as a resource to enrich science courses with a variety of aspects of the interaction of science, technology and society. A recent evaluation of the project[7] has shown that the materials have been well received by teachers and widely adopted for GCSE.

The SATIS project includes among its aims the intention to:

◊ show that science is not confined to the school laboratory, but is manifest in all aspects of the world, both local and distant.

> "The demands made on able pupils should be extended so that they are challenged not by the task of accumulating ever greater stores of scientific knowledge but by the applications of scientific principles to the real world, by the opportunity to investigate and to solve problems, and by the necessity of bringing scientific knowledge to bear on assignments where the answer cannot be predicted in advance."

◊ show the need to consider the impact of technological activity on the environment and the need for careful use of natural resources;

◊ develop awareness of the need for careful use of natural resources;

◊ show that science is not an isolated field of enquiry but interacts with other disciplines such as geography, economics and history;

◊ show that real-life decisions often have be to based on conflicting or inadequate information, that decisions involve compromise and that there is not always a 'right' answer[8] All of these aims can be met through units related to environmental education, as is shown in the next section.

## Teaching Methods

The DES Policy Statement calls for a variety of teaching approaches in science education which emphasize practical, investigative and problem-solving activities. It also states that:

*"The demands made on able pupils should be extended so that they are challenged not by the task of accumulating ever greater stores of scientific knowledge but by the applications of scientific principles to the real world, by the opportunity to investigate and to solve problems, and by the necessity of bringing scientific knowledge to bear on assignments where the answer cannot be predicted in advance."[9]*

Environmental education provided many opportunities for challenging students in these ways. The SATIS project has introduced teachers to a wider range of strategies. The project has identified existing good practice and allowed others to share in the innovative ideas contributed by the teachers who wrote the units.

SATIS units are intended to involve students as actively as possible. Instead of simply reading or listening, the units are designed to get students involved in comprehension questions, discussion, simulations, role-play, decision-making, problem solving, surveys and data analysis. Here are some examples:

*Unit 110 Hilltop*
*- an agricultural problem*
This is about a trace-element disease affecting farm animals; the activities include data analysis and problem solving.

*Unit 602 Limestone Inquiry*
This is a simulation into a public inquiry about a proposed quarry extension in the Peak District National Park. Groups of students have to represent different interest groups and make the case in the light of criteria laid down in legislation.

*Unit 807 Radiation -
how much do you get?*
The students use maps and tables from NRPB publications to estimate their own radiation dose from natural and artificial sources. They discuss the risks and the criteria used to draw up the recommended limits for radiation doses.

*Unit 901 The Chinese
Cancer Detectives*
This is a role-play exercise in which students work as a team of health-care specialists planning a programme of education for villagers in a Chinese valley where a combination of dietary and environmental factors contribute to a high level of oesophageal cancer.

*Unit 902 Acid Rain*
This is a structured discussion in which students are asked to decide what should be done to cut down on the effects of acid rain. Each group has a different briefing sheet dealing with a particular aspect of the problem.

The Nature Conservancy Council has suggested that:

"An important aim of environmental education is the development of analytical and critical skills so that people are able to arrive at their own independent opinions. Ideally these should be based on a balanced presentation of the facts and views of different people".[10]

The SATIS project has published a variety of units to show how this can be done.

**Coherence and progression**

Novel approaches to science education can bring their own problems. The cause of environmental education will not be served if students find themselves endlessly contemplating a limited range of topical issues such as acid rain, the hazards of nuclear waste and the destruction of tropical forests. We have to ensure that there is both co-operation between the various subject areas at each stage and progression from year to year.

We must seek to give students a sense of growing understanding of the world around them. At its simplest, this might start with young children exploring their immediate environment; then, as they get older, they can extend their investigations to national and global issues, using a variety of sources of information including books, magazines, videos and data bases.

We must avoid the danger of repeatedly confronting students with an increasing number of depressing stories about the despoliation of the planet Earth. We will not serve the cause of environmental education by engendering despair. As children grow to be young adults, they must also be given a sense of confidence and capability. They must explore the ways in which decisions about scientific and technological issues are taken in a democratic society. They must feel that as citizens they will be able to influence these decisions.

Clearly science teachers must collaborate with colleagues responsible for developing technological capability, economic and political awareness as well as literacy and numeracy. Environmental education is essentially interdisciplinary.
© Andrew Hunt, March 1988

**Conclusion**

Science courses have an important role to play in helping young people to develop their own insights into human behaviour and its effects on the environment. Current trends in science education are giving greater prominence to environmental issues. The Interim Report of the National Curriculum Science Working Group seems to endorse these trends. The outstanding task is to ensure a co-ordinated and progressive approach to environmental education across the curriculum throughout the years of compulsory education and beyond.

**References**
1 National Curriculum Science Working Group, *'Interim Report'* DES November 1987
2 IUCN & UNEP, *'An Introduction to the World Conservation Strategy'* 1984
3 Northern Examining Association,*' Science (Modular) Syllabus'* for the 1988 examination. The syllabus is being revised so that it will also lead to the new Science: Double award criteria.
4 Nuffield-Chelsea Curriculum Trust, *'Nuffield Co-ordinated Sciences'* to be published by Longman, April 1988
5 Nuffield Co-ordinated Sciences, *'Draft Syllabus prepared for submission to the Secondary Examinations Council'*.Nuffield-Chelsea Curriculum Trust, 1988
6 Secondary Science Curriculum Review, *'Better Science: making it relevant to young people'* Heinemann, 1987
7 Walker,D.R. *'The Evaluation of SATIS'* a limited edition to be published by the ASE for the SATIS project
8 Science and Technology in Society, *'General Guide for Teachers'* Association for Science Education, 1986
9 Department of Education and Science and Welsh Office, *'Science 5 - 15: A statement of policy"* HMSO, 1985,
10 Quoted from a Nature Conservancy Council leaflet introducing the *'Points of view'* series of information sheets.

# Art and environment

Photograph: Irene Reina Lengui

This is a synopsis of the book
'An Eye on the Environment'
written by Bev Joicey when
Adviser for Art Education in
Humberside LEA

# Art and environment

## Introduction

Increasingly there is a growing general awareness that the shape and nature of buildings and places affect the activities which go on within and around them. There is little doubt that the physical environment is a significant influence on both the objective and subjective world of the child. It is therefore important to help children develop an active awareness of their surroundings in order that they can better understand the influence it may be having on them. A function of education should be to help children acquire a language which enables them to recognize the environment. They need to be equipped with the knowledge and means to describe, analyse and evaluate the surrounding architecture, landscape, fauna and associated detail. They should be prepared to understand and communicate that which they are observing. The inter-relationship between the man-made world and the natural world, for example, is crucial to long term development and such progress implies that young people must have a conscious appreciation of what is taking place within and between the two.

## Aims

Intimate awareness of the environment can come from the sensory experience of being in the landscape. The arts can provide the language through which to understand that experience because the arts are primarily concerned with identifying and structuring elements which constitute the drama, mood and sensation of being in a place.

Art itself is made up of the discrete skills of drawing, painting, three-dimensional work and associated craft skills. These skills are often directed toward the visual interpretation of those elements which constitute the imaginative, emotional and sensory experience of being in a place. The technical development of these skills is best achieved through direct observation and interpreting those observations through selected media. In this way, the visual arts can provide a means through which a conscious relationship with the surrounding environment is achieved.

> "The aim of teaching awareness of the environment through art is both to help children better understand the world around them and, through that experience, the world within them."

The processes of art provide the opportunity to observe carefully and to reflect on that which is being seen in the light of previous experience. The mind retains while the eye gathers more information. As the language of art helps picture experience in the mind so the environment can continue to feed experience into that language. In this way, the visual arts can encourage the experience of seeing and of knowing. The aim of teaching awareness of the environment through art is both to help children better understand the world around them and, through that experience, the world within them. A major concern is to teach children to look and to see and to know.

## Objectives

The artistic process involves skills which can be used as a means of gathering, using and analysing visual information. The acquisition of appropriate skills is traditionally highly dependent on the child being asked to look at aspects of their personal environment and so the relationship of the visual arts to environmental education can be very much entwined. If the skills are genuinely acquired then they can become permanent tools for the process of learning and if learnt through closely observing the environment then the environment may remain a permanent source of interest. The child can retain the vocabulary of art for the rest of their life and use that vocabulary to continue the process of recording, using and analysing the physical world.

Drawing is a vital tool in developing these skills, in maintaining an awareness of the artistic process and in coming to terms with observation. Drawing a closely observed shrub, an aspect of some industrial complex or the sweep of a hillside can provide profound knowledge of the shape, form, structure and detail of the various elements which make up the source of observation. At the same time, the physical act of drawing provides scope for gaining awareness of the context in which the observed object exists, the effect of changing light on the shrub, the noise and action of industry and the sound of an empty hillside. The act of drawing offers the opportunity to reflect on that which is being drawn and general perception is increased.

Art activities are rarely exclusive and medium tends to grow into medium. It is as important to draw with colour as well as the more traditional media of pencil, graphite and charcoal, and as drawing in colour develops, reflections and sensations will emerge within the observations and the process of painting assert itself.

Three-dimensional work is another significant tool in becoming aware of a place and in acquiring a language of both analysis and expression. Recreating objects found and seen, places visited, imagined or observed, can provide further and alternative knowledge about form and structure, detail and shape. The experience of moulding and manipulating materials, building and restructuring materials to represent some aspect of the observed environment provides an excellent opportuntiy for the maker to consider how forms may effect the functions which take place within them. As models emerge and change so the ideas suggested by the shape and form change.

Other craft media can similarly offer opportunities to increase skill and awareness of the craft through careful attention to working from the environment. The visual and tactile qualities involved in the process of exploring observations through weaving and associated fabric work implies a sensitivity to texture and may highlight subtlety of colour. Printmaking with the implicit emphasis on flat colour and planes of light encourages those working within the media to look with a more apparently detached objectivity. At the same time, the making of books may grow from the progressive and systematic concern and the subsequent need to store, present and retrieve information. Such a process may imply the acquisition and development of particular skills, for example, involving detailed illustration, the making of paper and the binding of books.

The skills acquired by conscious observation through the media of the visual arts are likely to increase the sensibility of the observer and may open a sensitivity to the environment which will remain forever.

## The Process

A significant quality in the visual arts as a tool for learning is that it frequently places emphasis on children learning for themselves. The basic skills of the subject are comparatively easily acquired. The initial stages in drawing,

> "The skills acquired by conscious observation through the media of the visual arts are likely to increase the sensibility of the observer and may open a sensitivity to the environment which will remain forever"

painting and modelling come easily to the child and from them progress and development can be dependent upon presenting the child with stimulating materials or events or places. Much of this material is readily available within the environment and the subject area is traditionally associated with observing both the natural and man-made world. The process is simple. The child is asked to look at a particular plant, a collection of objects or machinery, an animal or place and, as the first marks are made, the child is able to compare those marks with the reality of the object observed. It is the object which informs the child whether the drawing, painting or model is succeeding or not and they can continually assess their progress by comparing their work with the original. In many respects, the environment can become the teacher, though the success of this process is highly dependent on the selective intervention of the teacher in identifying appropriate subject matter and maintaining an atmosphere of commitment.

This approach provides the circumstances for learning, much

more than the symbolising of reality on a piece of paper, or for conveying the feelings and reactions to being in a place or reacting to an object. Drawing plant formations, environmental structures, towns or landscapes is an excellent means through which the child can acquire a range of knowledge. Accurate observation on a small or large scale involves the process of selecting from a range of possibilities, and extracting appropriate information. It may involve having to identify patterns, appreciate, record and make judgements about difference and similarity. Following the lines of a building structure, tracing the pattern of fields, carefully drawing the windows in a building or cogs in a machine all involve the children in using knowledge so acquired in combination with personal feeling and response so that judgment can be both rational and individual.

The direction of learning can take its own course. In the case of a beach pebble, the child may become aware and take an interest in rock structure as a result of drawing the object or they may simply enjoy recreating the quality of surface texture. Alternatively, the pebble may evoke memories of beach holidays to be recreated or it may become a starting point for drawings which lead to paintings of imaginative landscape which lead to models of cliff dwellings, fairy grottoes or the home of some phantasy creature.

The key to success with this approach lies with the objects to be used as starting points, the attitudes of the pupils and the experience of the teacher. The objects must excite curiosity and stretch the observational powers of the children. If this is achieved the children will approach their learning with a positive and enthusiastic attitude. Making the first mark is important and knowledge of technique and skill will affect this but enthusiasm can override difficulties. If the subject of attention can excite the commitment and interest of the children then the problem of making that first mark will be overcome. Source material is crucial in this process. It must excite and arouse the interest of the children. It must provide scope for a range of learning to take place. Working from the environment achieves this.

## Conclusion

The environment is the ring around the individual which consists of the objects, places, influences and conditions which shape them. Similarly, it is the ring around society. If education is about providing the languages and experiences which help the individual understand who and what they are and how they can develop, then a major starting point must be the identification of the environment. The visual arts provide a significant means in helping to achieve this, creating shape and form out of something apparently very ordinary. As the written and spoken work can help systemize experience in the mind so the visual arts provide the means to picture experience. A place needs to be visually recorded in order for it to be recognized and understood. Therefore the environment without art may be a place without context.

© Bev Joicey, March 1988

# Environmental education in religious education

Photograph: Helen Tann

Sandra Palmer
Lecturer in Religious Education
Manchester Polytechnic

# Environmental education in religious education

## Introduction

This is a background paper with suggestions for the place and content of environmental education within religious education. It looks at:
1. the relationship between religion and our understanding of the environment;
2. the educational context;
3. the aims and objectives for the environmental content within religious education bearing in mind the relationship between the two and the educational context;
4. recommendations and suggestions for the content to further these aims and objectives.

## 1. The relationship between religion and the understanding of the environment

### Perception

In order to understand the role religion has to make in our understanding of the environment, it is fundamental to acknowledge first that none of us are impartial, uninvolved observers of our environment.

We each bring our own perspective and give the environment meaning and significance in our own terms. As Soskice so eloquently puts it:

"*man, like the spider, spins out of himself the world which he inhabits*". (Janet Martin Soskice, page 80 '*Metaphor and Religious Language*' Clarendon Press, Oxford 1985).

We cannot know phenomena as they are in themselves; indeed in the Jewish, Islamic and Christian traditions that is a prerogative which belongs only to God. We impose a framework on the world with a sense of our own place within it; otherwise we would not be able to act.

When we perceive a phenomenon, whether it be directly or indirectly through a picture or an idea of it, we are bringing ourselves into a relationship with it.

How we perceive a phenomenon affects our relationship with it and therefore how we respond to it.

These three aspects of perception are illustrated in the way two children react to the same dog. The first child sees the dog as something that might leap at him and knock him over or even bite. This perception leads to a relationship of fear between the child and dog. His response is to shrink behind his mother. The second

> "We each bring our own perspective and give the environment meaning and significance in our own terms."

child views the animal as a big warm cuddly object of friendship. Her relationship with it is one of love. Her response is to rush forward and stroke it. In each instance the perception has affected the relationship and in turn the response.

### The role of religion in perception

Many variables interacting on each other make up the lens through which we see the world: our personal experiences, the demands of our sources of livelihood and pleasure, the examples set by family and peers.

A major variable is that of our culture. Our perception of the rights of the individual, privacy, time, the environment (the list is endless), are all coloured by our culture. Linked inexorably with cultures are the religions which have helped to mould them.

All religions have within them implicit and explicit teachings about the environment. Where a religion has been the main faith of a society, those ideas help shape the perceptions at a pre-cognitive level, even of those who do not subscribe to the faith. So much so that these perceptions are often taken for granted and presumed to be the only way there is to see.

The eminent Hindu politician and environmentalist Dr. Karan Singh made clear how much religious background affects the way we see by contrasting Christian/Western perceptions of the natural world with that of the Hindu, when he addressed the 25th aniversary conference of the World Wide Fund for Nature in Assisi. He reminded the delegates of the headlines in Britain the day of the Queen's coronation:

"Hilary conquers Everest."
Were man and mountain at war with each other that one should be pronounced the victor?

Not to the Hindu, pointed out Dr. Singh, for the Hindu believes that everything is one. We are all part of one whole, and seeking to live in harmony with the whole, not pulling against it. But 'yes', they are at war, according to the Western press and most Western minds. To many in the West the natural environment must be mastered and put to the best use for mankind.

The contrast in attitudes was also seen in the actions of the two men who reached the summit first. Edmund Hilary, a Christian, planted a flag, the symbol of a victor. Sherpa Tenzing, a Hindu, knelt in awe. The cultural perception of each resulted in different behaviour.

Many of the environmentalists attending the conference were taken aback. They had assumed that their's was the only way to see.

A second example is the way the relationship between man and animals is seen in different cultures.

In mainstream Christian/Western thought animals are ontologically different to man, and this way of thinking includes those who see men and animals as having common ancestors. Animals do not have rights and they are unable to make moral judgements. In

> **"All religions have within them implicit and explicit teachings about the environment."**

Christian thought only man has the ability to distinguish between good and evil. This distinction is manifest in the way the animal population is managed. The culling of a herd, to bring it back into its numerical balance with its habitat, is regarded as good environmental practice in the West, whereas the culling of a human population is not morally acceptable.

In contrast, in Hindu thought man and animals are ontologically at one. They are linked together by a continuing cycle of reincarnation. Each one must fulfil the 'dharma' (duty) of its incarnation in order to receive a favourable 'Karma' or rebirth in the next.

### *Environmental Teaching within a Faith*

Christianity is a clear example of how a religion has within it both implicit and explicit teachings about the environment. Christianity is man-centred. Its central themes are about the condition of man, his relationship with God and his salvation. Implicit in this is that the world is of secondary importance, and indeed there has often been in Christianity a denial of the physical world in favour of the spiritual. There are also explicit teachings, most significantly in the myth of the creation of the first

man Adam. He is created separately to the rest of creation, and has authority and dominion over it. In the way this story from Genesis is usually told the world is there for his use.

Christianity also illustrates how a religion may have within it a number of theologies and teachings, but some come to the fore in particular cultural contexts and others may be peripheral or lie dormant.

Within Christianity there is a tradition which has been neglected by much of Western Protestant Christendom. It is that God's love extends beyond man to the whole of creation and that while man has an honoured place within the natural world, creation glorifies God in its own right. This is a theme running through the Psalms, most explicit in Psalm 148, and also in Job where man is reminded of how small and insignificant he is compared to the power of God and the vastness of creation.

There are a number of stories about saints who taught this belief exemplifying it in their own lives. The outstanding one is St. Francis of Assisi.

But in this tradition it is not just that God loves the world, but in His love He shares its suffering and agony. The legend of St. Hubert is one which clothes this belief.

Hubert was a king who enjoyed hunting. One Good Friday, much to the dismay of his servants, he set out to hunt deer. After a fine chase he trapped a magnificent stag in a clearing. The animal stood frozen with fear. Hubert drew back his arrow, but then as he took his sights he saw between the antlers of the deer the stretched out figure of Christ. He fell to the ground, and gave up hunting. In the anguish of the deer Hubert had seen the anguish of Christ.

### *The Effect of Religious Perception on Reaction to the Environment*

Like all variables which contribute to our perception, religion affects the way we treat the environment. The different behaviour of Christian and Hindu at the top of Everest has already been noted.

The way land is utilized is another example. When land is seen as inert, something to be exploited to the full, then it can be pumped full of chemicals and overused. Where it is seen as a mother it is loved and nurtured, as man has sought to live in harmony with it. Western environmentalists are now arguing that the former is not sensible, but their justifications are still on the basis that it is not good for man, rather than a view of the environment as a whole.

### *Summary*

Religion affects the way we see the world, understand our place in it and therefore how we behave towards it. Through example, story, folklore, ritual (secular and religious), each generation learns to share the perceptions of its forefathers until they are challenged by encounter with another view.

### 2. The educational context

◊ Britain is a pluralist society with children of a number of religions and of no religion. However, Christianity is the faith that has most shaped the perceptions of British culture and also is the faith which has the most adherents in this country. Its celebrations and rituals of passage are shared by the majority even of those who would not call themselves believers.

> **"God's love extends beyond man to the whole of creation"**

◊ Modern educational philosophy encourages the learner to be autonomous in his learning and to think for himself. Implicit in this is that he should be open to change which might result in a radical shift of position or in a modification of view. This entails a willingness to learn from others.

Religious education has been one of the last disciplines to take on board this critical openness. In many instances there has been a fear that the true faith will become corrupted.

It is important to recognize, though, that religions do not exist in a vacuum. They are in a symbiotic relationship with the cultures in which they are embodied, moulding them but in turn being shaped themselves by historical events, economics. and the other religions and philosophies with which they come into contact. The Old Testament writers Daniel and Ezekiel drew on images from the Babylonian religions. Buddhism has taken different forms as it has taken root in different parts of Asia depending largely on local practices already established. The Christian Fathers used the neo-platonist categories of Greek philosophers to articulate their faith; indeed Christianity has a long history of taking already established religious rituals and making them Christian, for instance mid-Winter solstice into Christmas.

◊ The link between moral education and religious education has always been strong. It is within R.E. that moral questions have been deliberately raised and discussed and it is to R.E. that public and government have turned to raise children into responsible citizens.

## 3. Aims and objectives of an environmental component within religious education

These aims and objectives have been drawn up on the following bases:

◊ Given the role of perspective in our understanding of the environment and the role of religion in forming that perspective, environmental education within R.E. is about **how** the environment is understood (see section 1).

◊ Such education would encourage the children to think for themselves about the subject but be willing to learn from others (see section 2).

◊ In the context of R.E., environmental studies would involve the raising of moral issues about man's relationship with the environment, with the recognition that different religious pespectives will affect the way such issues are discussed.

---

**"We have already in our schools a festival about the environment which remains popular. It is, of course, Harvest Festival."**

---

The environmental crisis the world faces with the destruction of rainforests disturbing weather patterns, the erosion of the ozone layer, the pollution of the seas and soil, poses moral problems for all the earth's inhabitants, with short term personal needs and wants often coming into conflict with overall needs.

But these global environmental problems are not the only moral questions. There are also questions related to the rights of animals versus the rights of humans, an individual's right to do what he likes to the environment where he lives versus that of his community, and many more.

Moreover, it is possible to have a great deal of knowledge, an extensive understanding of the environment, and not care a thing about it, but to use one's knowledge to one's own selfish ends. After all a poacher has to have an intimate knowledge of his prey's habitat and habits in order to pursue his sport successfully. In contrast, someone with a very simplistic scientific view may have a deep

love of the environment. In the classroom, the furtherance of an understanding of the environment should be coupled with an encouragement to the commitment of its welfare.

*Aims*
◊ that children will develop understanding of **how** the environment can be understood.
◊ that they will learn to make a moral response to the environment, putting the needs of the whole before personal need and want.

*Objectives in practice*
Objectives are given together with recommendations and examples of how they can be put into practice. In many instances what aids one objective also aids another. Obviously the level tackled would need to be appropriate to the age, ability and experiences of the children. As Christianity is the formative faith of Britain, I recommend that it is given special attention, but that a wide variety of faiths should be drawn on both to increase an understanding of perspective but also because many have something of value to say.

*Objective 1… that children will recognize that they bring to the environment and its components their own perspective which is one of many, and this perspective affects the way they act towards the environment.*
◊ Simply asking the children how they feel about different animals and places is likely to throw up a number of different perspectives even within the one class. This would also include the children articulating their attitudes which could lead to debate of the moral issues, e.g. Is a spider friend or foe? Should it be killed or not?
◊ Looking at animals from the perspective of different people's needs and experience, e.g. Does the vegetable grower see the rabbits in the garden the same way as

his city guest? How would the two differ in their behaviour towards rabbits?

◊ Learning that perceptions may vary from culture to culture by looking at the way different groups regard animals. Which animals are acceptable as food or pets differs from culture to culture and similarly the character which is imparted to them varies. In England, for instance, the owl is viewed as the wise old bird, accentuated by the good press it has received in A.A. Milne's "Winnie the Pooh". In many parts of Africa such as Nigeria, where it is called the witch bird, it is an evil omen. Again, how do these different perceptions affect behaviour?

◊ With the older age groups larger and more abstract phenomena can be looked at, such as ways of viewing time. Western story and speech takes for granted a linear view of time in contrast to the cyclical view of Eastern faiths. For one, the story of the universe continues to unfold but only exists once; for the other, this world, this universe is but one of many which will have its existence for a time but will be destroyed and then come into being again in a never-ending cycle.

*Objective 2 ... that children will critically analyse the roots of these perspectives, their own and others'*

◊ By reflecting on the experiences that have built their own perspective, e.g. Why am I frightened of dogs?

◊ By examining what lies behind the perspective of different groups and how this affects their response. Why might a vegetable farmer reach for his gun when he sees a rabbit?

◊ This examination of the roots of perspective should include an analysis of how stories affect perception and how stories have developed. One activity for example could be to look at how different animals have been portrayed in cartoons. Do the children think this has affected the way they think about these animals? Another would be to draw up character references for different animals based on legends around the world.

I would recommend that stories which have been particularly formative in a faith should receive special attention. These would include the main creation stories from the different world religions.

*Objective 3 ... that children will be willing and able to learn from perspectives other than their own.*

◊ Looking at the area in the light of another's needs, for instance writing a guide to the local area as it provides for the needs of an old person; looking to see how certain species of animals are catered for in the area; assessing how any potential change such as the building of a car park or new block of flats would affect various inhabitants both human and animal.

◊ Attempting to look at an area through radically different eyes, for example writing a diary or letter home as if one of the Bishnoi of North-west India. These people are often known as the tree huggers because of the high status of trees in their religion. Such an exercise would obviously necessitate the children being well-informed about the Bishnoi people, but would also involve the children thinking again and valuing the function of trees.

◊ Hearing and discussing stories from a number of traditions: stories can ask the listener to empathize with an entirely different point of view and thus to 'think again'. Story-telling in all faiths has always been a means not only of passing on the faith but of confronting the listener, hence the wide use of stories by religious leaders. The Buddhist Jataka tales are one group of such legends in their demonstration of the love of the Buddha for his fellow beings.

It is recommended that, in particular, there should be a widening of the range of stories children are exposed to from the Christian tradition, reflecting the different strands within it.

◊ Looking at familiar stories through another's eyes. Jews, Christians and Muslims all share the same creation stories, on the surface. Protestant Christians in the United States have used the stories in Genesis as a justification for the exploitation of the earth, and I have already argued that they have contributed to Western man's understanding of his rights over the natural world.

Orthodox Jews tell the same story. They share the view that man is distinct from the rest of creation and he is to use the world for his own enjoyment, but he is also to manage it wisely. He is to tend and care for it, replenishing its stocks, not working it to the point of exhaustion or even death. Both traditions draw on the same story of creation from Genesis 1 and 2, but over the centuries their stories have diverged only slightly but nevertheless significantly in terms of the role they give to man in his rights over the natural world.

*Objective 4 ... that children will want to care for the environemnt*

◊ In any class in Britain there are likely to be children whose families are practising members of a faith. Some of these children will be keen believers; many others may return to the faith as adults. For such people, adherence to the moral precepts of their religion is important. They should be at least aware about the positive teachings on the environment within their own faith, some of which may be lying dormant.

◊ In the Primary school, where the class teacher has responsibility for all or nearly all disciplines, these R.E. objectives provide a hidden curriculum for the way he/she teaches science. Such scientific projects as tending a school garden, recording the seasonal changes in a local park, taking care of a class pet can all lead to a love of the environment and therefore a desire to care for it. (The last example can of course be counter-productive if the animal is

kept under bad conditions.)
◊ Stories have again a special role, as indeed does anything which invites empathy, for it can lead to love and care.
◊ There is also a place for a call to a response in an explicitly religious context, and this place may be in the form of a festival, bearing in mind that the number of festivals celebrated in British schools is on the increase even though the attention to the festival may be as little as one afternoon. Festivals are a means of handing on the teaching of the faith, but they are far more than this. To begin with, they are usually, although not always, a time for celebration. Something in the faith, whether a belief, an important person or an event in its history, has given cause for rejoicing. A commitment to the welfare of the environment presupposes that it is worth caring about, both as a whole and in its many parts and if it is worth caring about, it is a cause for rejoicing.

In the Judaeo-Christian tradition festivals may be also the time of a reminder of covenants between God and man. The covenant is an agreement between God and man in which man has rights but also responsibilities. The drama and symbol of the festival celebration draw the participants in, exhorting them to renew their part in the covenant. The food and liturgy of the Passover meal, for instance, is making present the events of the past and makes the existential demand of those celebrating that they should live as the people of God in every respect. Easter is for many Christians the time for a renewal of the vows of baptism.

We have already in our schools a festival about the environment which remains popular. It is, of course, Harvest Festival. At the moment it is generally very man-orientated, thanking God for what the earth has provided for man and praying for those whom the earth seems to have failed. While this does not negate the validity of these acts there is the potential to transform Harvest Festival into a time when the children celebrate the natural world, think about their role and responsibility towards it, and are encouraged to a commitment to it through the symbol and drama of the festival.

The 1987 Harvest Festival at Winchester Cathedral stands as a model for such festivals. It was a Christian festival but there were people of other faiths, participating as appropriate, and indeed the liturgy is at present being adapted by a number of Jewish congregations. It climaxed with a call to commitment to the environment, symbolized by the tying of rainbow coloured threads around the wrist of a neighbour. It is a symbol that could easily be adapted for school children but there is also plenty of scope for children, to create their own.
© Sandra Palmer, March 1988

## Conclusion

This paper has made suggested aims and objectives for environmental education in religious education on the basis of the particular contribution an appreciation of the relationship between religion and the environment has to make to an understanding of the environment. Moreover, environmental education should be a key part of Religious Education to further the aims and objectives of that subject.
◊ It furthers an understanding of the role religions play in the lives of their followers and the cultures in which they exist.
◊ Teachings about man's place in the world and his responsibility towards it are central to all religions as has been argued in the section on the educational context. Thus they should be central to any study of a particular faith.
◊ An awareness of self is an objective which is articulated in the majority of modern R.E. agreed syllabuses. A critical study of the role and makeup of perception must lead to a greater understanding of the self.
In short, a curriculum for either religious or environmental studies which ignored the link between the two would be inadequate. Such a link is of mutual benefit to both and indeed of fundamental importance to both disciplines.

**Bibliography**

Global Environmental Education Project,'Earthwatch Now',
Richmond Publishing Co. Ltd with WWF, 1986
'Worlds of Difference' pupils book, teachers book and wallcharts,
Blackies and Pictorial Charts Educational Trust and WWF, 1984
Palmer M. 'Genesis or Nemesis - belief, meaning and ecology' Dryad Press.1988

# Challenge and commitment: music in school and society

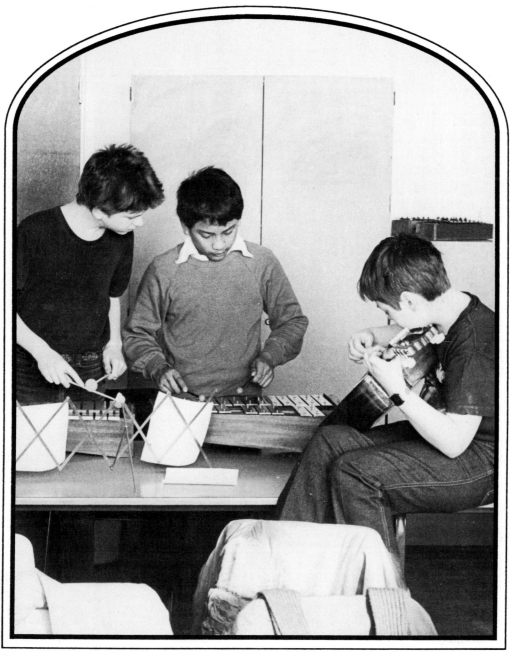

Photograph: Keith Hawkins

Professor John Paynter
Department of Music
University of York

# Challenge and commitment: music in school and society

Change in education is a slow process. Old convictions die hard, and teachers whose work points in different directions normally find themselves part of a vulnerable minority. Just occasionally, however, something occurs that draws together all the diverse effort for change and gives it formal approval.

> "Traditionally, the content of the average school music lesson has been regarded at best as a cultural additive"

Ths is what has happened with the arrival of the GCSE. For once, it would seem, the old jibe that "*When two or three are gathered together to change a syllabus, lo it shall remain as it always was*" has not been applicable. The determination to revise the examination process at 16+ brought about a nationwide reappraisal, not only of how we assess what is learned, but also (and perhaps more importantly) of what school is for, and why certain bodies of knowledge and experience should find a place in the curriculum at all.

Currently, the subject criteria for the GCSE are stimulating significant changes of approach throughout all areas of the Secondary school curriculum; this will quickly affect the whole spectrum from the primary school to higher education. Nowhere in the GCSE criteria has the change been more dramatic than in what is now specified for Music.

Nevertheless, compared with the pros and cons of other curriculum matters, the news that there has been a revolution in music education seems unlikely to cause much of a stir;- and the reason is not hard to find. In spite of the fact that music manifestly plays an important role in so many aspects of life and few people get through a day without hearing some music somewhere, its contribution to general education has not been noticeably valued; no doubt because for so long it has been regarded principally as an activity mainly for the talented.

Traditionally, the content of the average school music lesson has been regarded at best as a 'cultural additive': a process which might inject a few facts of musical theory and history, but which would have to leave direct involvement with the artistic excitement of music to those best able to cope with it outside the classroom.

Responsibility for that view lies not so much with those teaching music as with the system in which they teach. 'Schooling' is hedged about with expectations based, as often as not, upon unquestioned assumptions. For example, it is anticipated that children will spend most of their time in school receiving information from other people. Opportunities to develop their own ideas or their powers of creativity and inventiveness are likely to be limited because it is assumed that the main task of education is to impart established facts and time-hallowed opinions.

First come I, my name is Jowett.
There's no knowledge but I know it.
I am Master of this college:
What I don't know isn't knowledge. [1]

This is a process we inherit from our Victorian ancestors, although they themselves were not oblivious of its faults, as is evident from H. C. Beeching's light-hearted tilt at his distinguished mentor Benjamin Jowett, Master of Balliol and Regius Professor of Greek.

In an educational scheme dominated by the idea of teachers passing on information, even music was forced to conform if the subject was to retain curriculum respectability. In particular, it was difficult to see how music-making (other than massed singing) could be accommodated in school classrooms. Thus choirs, bands and orchestras were labelled 'extra-curricular' and 'recreational' and found no place in the time-table.

Gradually all that has changed. What now emerges as criteria for Music in the GCSE is to a large extent the distillation of a vast amount of classroom experiment which, little by little over the past twenty-five years, has been refined into a new philosophy for music in education. The basic tenets are that music must be part of general education for all school students, not merely for a talented minority; that what is 'academic' about music (and therefore justifies its place in the educational process) is to be found in the experience of music making not in second-hand information about music.

For the essence of music is that it demands involvement, commitment and imagination; it is a creative art in all its modes: composing, performing and listening. In 1967, the composer R. Murray Schafer, one of the most persuasive advocates for a reawakening in music education, wrote:

> One learns practically nothing about the functioning of music by sitting in mute surrender before it ...
> one learns about sound only by making sound; about music only by making music. [2]

Two things in particular have characterised the dramatic changes of approach. Firstly, widening access to instrumental lessons and to performing opportunities in classroom music as well as in the out-of-timetable ensembles and Youth Orchestras; secondly, emphasis upon children composing their own music.

The latter is of particular significance because it takes us immediately to the heart of the creative process. "Creativity" is a word which has, perhaps, been overworked in education and to some extent discredited by misuse and misunderstanding. This is unfortunate because it is still the principal clue to the educational importance of the aesthetic areas of the curriculum. Creativity implies origination and invention; but it goes beyond that to include interpretation and 'personalised' imitation. And, whether the action is interpretative or inventive, creativity involves commitment to preference, choice and decision. Its concern is within dependent, imaginative responses to events, ideas and the means of expression; thus it differs substantially from activities which are rule-directed or based mainly upon objectively acquired information.

Music lends itself to inventiveness more readily than any other means of expression - which may explain its universal appeal and variety. It is an entirely 'free' medium which, unlike other forms of art, has no obvious links with the observable, measurable realities of existence. By association it may, for some, evoke feelings and even images, but the nature of such a response is, in any case, different for each listener because music does not communicate in a discursive or linguistic fashion with one-to-one meanings.

Principally music 'describes' time; not time as the clock marks it but time as we perceive it passing, in different ways according to our moods or circumstances. The expressive qualities of music which delight and move us are directly related to the way in which the musical ideas 'go on' in time; the satisfaction we receive from performing or listening to music derives in the main from the feeling of completeness or wholeness in the 'model of time' which the sounds and their organisation create.

Whether we notate it carefully on paper or create it live through what is sometimes called 'empirical composition', making up a piece of music always throws us back upon our innermost

> "All over the world, for as far back in history as anthropologists can take us, people have invented music and preserved musical traditions."

resources, because solutions to the problems of structure are revealed not through what other people may tell us to do but through our sensitivity to the sounds and to our own musical ideas. It may be an individual exploration or a group activity (as is frequently the case in jazz and in some non-western musics, where the process is often akin to the productiveness of a 'brain-storming' discussion), but the principle is the same. Possibilities must be examined; problems and solutions tried out; preferred routes confirmed by frequent repetition: judging carefully, as we go along, how certain ideas - melodies, rhythmic patterns, combinations of instrumental or vocal 'colour', and so on - can be extended, developed, transformed or should give way to fresh thoughts. The prime considerations are: 'How should the music begin? How should it go on and for how long? How should it finish?'

No externally imposed rules can answer such questions. Every piece of music is a new adventure in sound and time.It is a process of thinking and making through which - almost without realising it - we become intensely aware of things that matter to us; of our commitment to ideas and our determination to see the task through to the end and to stand by the decisions we have taken. These feelings are all the more powerful because we are dealing with the abstract materials of musical sound. We shall not be inhibited by the demands of an objective view; but, by the same token, there is no excusing the product for being almost but not quite like an identifiable model, because music has no such direct points of reference outside itself. Each sound-structure has to 'work' by commending itself to us when we listen to it in its completed form. Of course, there may be other factors such as words or titles. Even so, the success of the music lies in the use of the **musical** ideas, whatever additional purpose those ideas may serve.

In school music education, we now have a substantial background of creative work stretching back for more than a quarter of a century. Internationally the literature on this subject is extensive, although much of the pioneer work was done in Great Britain and Brtitish teachers have continued to lead the world in developing the techniques of improvisation and composition, with related performance and listening, as classroom activities. The starting point is simple aural awareness: an appreciation of the soundscape around us and of the expressive potential of sounds. From there, pupils can develop at their own pace; sometimes working individually, sometimes in small groups of about five or six, learning through experience to relate sounds, ideas and structures, to create their own music and their interpretations of other people's music.

All over the world, for as far back in history as anthropologists can take us, people have invented music and preserved musical traditions. While the circumstances of making and presenting music, the cultural conventions and the learning processes vary immensely from one part of the world to another, the essential reality of music **remains the experience of its sounds.** In Britain, and elsewhere within similar educational systems, we have successfully evolved a rationale for music in schools which capitalises upon this essential experience, and by so doing broadens the scope and educational potential of the subject.

> **"The arts do not have a monopoly of creativity, but palpably they stand for an innovative view of the world."**

Uncertainty about the role of music in the school curriculum has been part of the larger problem of the place of arts generally. As we have seen, this has been compounded by a tendency to assume the necessity for a curriculum hierarchy in which areas of factual information, emphasising verbal or numerical expression, take precedence over non-verbal subjects such as art and music. Yet we know that, for the most part, individuals relate to their world both objectively, in clinical and absolute terms, and subjectively, through the indefinable but no less important mental processes of emotions.

Not only have we been slow to come to terms with these important differences but also, it would seem, we have been prepared to countenance attempts to side-step the problem by avoiding the distinctions altogether. Thus, new subject titles stressed practicality and usefulness; in this way we saw the visual arts turned into 'design'.

Music, of course, could not so easily be converted! While some might have wished to see it removed completely, it has maintained its position and, in a sense, now speaks most forcibly for the unique qualities of the affective curriculum. For, just as subjects which require a linear approach to

learning make an essential contribution in their own way to the totality of general education, so the arts, representing a very different, holistic way of 'coming to know', offer pupils something which would not otherwise be available.

Robert Witkin [3] has demonstrated that schooling which neglects "the intelligence of feeling" educates only half the child. Langer [4] reminds us that our existence is fundamentally sensory and that those powerful processes do not lend themselves easily to expression in "word-bound thought". It is for this reason that artistic creativity has such an important part to play in education, heightening our perceptions of the totality of the world and of the range of relationships we have with it. To attempt to make concrete, in a poem, a dance or a piece of music, those perceived but intangible relationships is to heighten self-perception and to see afresh the value of what is perceived about self and environment: people, places, ideas and the scope for action.

The school curriculum must be seen to provide a satisfactory balance between affirmative and innovative education. On the one hand, society needs to affirm and confirm its cultural heritage. On the other hand, we should be aware of the subtle changes in the world around us, be able to understand the responsibilities that life presents, and be equipped to react with sensitivity and imagination. The arts do not have a monopoly of creativity, but palpably they stand for an innovative view of the world. Above all, their processes of thinking and making highlight

elements of risk and challenge which are of such importance to those who must build society's future.

It is all too easy to lose sight of this. The quite proper and necessary quest for standards in education can, if we are not careful, place undue emphasis upon the passing of examinations rather than upon the curriculum content which examinations should consolidate. Expectations may then lean towards more and more certification, so that education takes on an 'appeasing' role, satisfying ambition with nothing more than a proliferation of degrees and diplomas: laurels upon which to rest.

Clearly, academic achievement must be appropriately rewarded, but the inherent dangers of the procedure should alert us to ensure that schools nurture in everyone the ability to deal with new and unfamiliar ideas and with the inevitable changes that lie ahead. As much as anything we need an education of challenge. Naturally, that applies across the whole curriculum; but it is especially evident in artistic enterprise within which the infinitely varied creative potential of music-making is so easily accessible to anyone willing to meet the challenge of 'putting sounds together'. It is an opportunity we cannot afford to miss.

© John Paynter, 1988

**References**

1 Beeching H.C. *The Masque of Balliol'* composed by, and circulated among members of, Balliol College, Oxford, during the 1870s.

2 Schafer R.M. *'Ear Cleaning: notes for an experimental music course'* BMI Canada Limited (1967), page 1. Reissued in Schafer R.M. *The Thinking Ear: complete writings on music education'* Arcana Editions, 1986.

3 Witkin R.W. *The Intelligence of Feeling'* London. Heinemann Educational, 1974.

4 Langer S.K. *'Philosophy in a New Key'* Cambridge Ma. Harvard University Press, page 260, (third edition, 1969)

# The word and the wilderness: environmental education within the english syllabus

Photograph: Nick Skinner

Jill Pirrie
Head of English
Halesworth Middle School

# The word and the wilderness: environmental education within the english syllabus

Environmental education, while not usually explicitly identified within an English syllabus, is inseparable from it. Moral attitudes and aesthetic values are more effectively inculcated than taught and this is the special property of fable, myth, poetry and story. This implies a strong measure of rote learning - the acceptable rote learning which has its roots deep within our culture and finds expression within each generation in the repetition of fable, myth, poetry and story until familiarity breeds the awareness which is the basis of true knowledge. This is our heritage. It is the means by which we attain to the self-knowledge which aspires to maturity. Only then can we turn outward into relationships which accept the responsibility incumbent on each one of us for the people, places, creatures of Planet Earth.

It is all so much a matter of learning to look, and language is inescapably a part of this process. The young child's first explorations of his immediate environment are confirmed and realised in his first tentative searching for the right word. The linking of the Name with the Thing becomes a moment of identification which can develop into a mutual recognition, a moment of empathy. Ted Hughes' "*Full Moon and Little Frieda*", for instance, captures his small daughter in a moment of acute awareness:

*"And you listening.*
*A spider's web, tense for the dew's touch,*
*A pail lifted, still and brimming..."*

There is tension here, a receptiveness which explodes into newly acquired language:

*"Moon!" you cry suddenly, "Moon! Moon!"*

And the new word initiates a mutual recognition:

*"The moon has stepped back like an artist gazing*
                                                *amazed at a work*
*That points at him amazed."*

It is the business of English teachers to nurture this amazement through developing the kind of language experiences which heighten the commonplace things of ordinary life. George Tardios speaks of a universal human sickness in his poem "*Images (Cyprus 1961)*" when he says:

*"The world is troubled*
*With a lack of looking"*.

And it is all too easy for childlike amazement to degenerate into an apathy in which the essential excitement is lost - excitement which is, at the same time, a coming to terms with environment and the tension by which the impulse to write is released.

For the very young the intensity of concentrated observation is entirely natural and unconscious. Timothy Rogers' anthology of poems composed by children aged two to eight years confirms this, often in startling images. Among many others there is the almost matter of fact:

*"The owl is the mother of the dark,*
*And the moon comes up*
*From under the mud."*

spoken by three year old Patrick Buxton. His mother writes this explanatory note:
*"Patrick was quiet in the back seat, and we thought he was asleep, when he suddenly said this in a funny sing-song little voice. It fitted the loneliness and desolation and general queerness of Bodmin Moor in that stormy light so well that I have never forgotten it."*
There is, however, a chilling postscript from the adult Patrick when he reports he has:
*"written nothing of any merit since."*
This statement is not just an indictment of a society which denigrates the highest expression of language in its clearest, most disciplined form of poetry, but also an indictment of a society which slowly but surely alienates us from the deep roots of our culture through which we come to terms with this wilderness Earth into which we are born. To deny our links with the wilderness is to deny our humanity.

In that moment on Bodmin Moor a three year old responded so fittingly to the place and the mood that his words were memorable. It is the English teacher's dilemma to focus on this childlike vision and help it to survive the coming of consciousness. Without consciousness the writer cannot aspire to mastery of his craft; without the childlike vision he has nothing important to say. W. Hart-Smith says in his poem "*Observation*":

*"Now and then concentrating*
*on the very small,*

*focusing my attention*
*on a very small area*
.............................................
*Someone seeing me*

*Staring so fixedly*
*at nothing*

*Might be excused*
*for thinking me vague, abstracted,*

*lost in introspection.*
*No! I am awake, absorbed,*
*just looking in a different direction."*

It is this kind of wakefulness, absorption, which is not just the hallmark of the poet, but of the mind liberated by language into an encounter with:

"*this crack in sandstone*"

or

"*moss, liverwort and fern*"

And, of course, the key words are:

"*just looking in a different direction.*"

It is only then that we find the extraordinary within the ordinary and our own experience is realised and externalised in language.

Perhaps it is the coming of consciousness from ten plus which is the greatest challenge to the teacher of English. When a very young child writes, or indeed speaks, about a landscape or a creature, he has no memory bank to draw upon; it is very much a matter for the moment. From ten plus (perhaps earlier) there is reflection, introspection, before the words are written. In "*Poetry in the Making*" Ted Hughes says this:

"*It is as if what they (children) know well can only become imagination, and available to the pen, when they have somehow left it.*"

This is to speak of the necessary detachment of the artist following the moment of intense involvement. It does not mean that children must be encouraged to write about what they do not know at close hand. It is within their immediate environment that they will find inspiration - but only if they are enabled to look as though for the first time with all the surprise and excitement of the toddler meeting the moon and naming it in a moment of explosive and delighted recognition. An encounter is disturbing because it initiates a relationship; a relationship implies a responsibility. To write imaginatively about our environment is, by the very nature of the activity, to become disturbed. Moreover, the piece of writing itself will be disturbing. It must be if the reader is to make that vital connection within the text, have that crucial moment of recognition/identification. All this is the very antithesis of that complacency which is the mark of our consumer-orientated society. Ted Hughes, again, has this to say of landscape:

"*And this is what makes landscapes valuable to us: not simply the presence of the elements; but the encounter between the elemental things and the living, preferably the human. It is ...
the presence of human feeling, what human feeling makes us conscious of.*"

This is well illustrated in the following extract from a poem written by a twelve year old Suffolk boy about a local wood. He sees the fallen tree and Uncle George sharing some deep and elemental source. In their ending the old man and the tree had become fused. They had shared the same life source; the same sun had shone upon them. The same rain had fallen upon them; the same earth had nurtured them. Now both had returned to their beginnings:

"*The death of Uncle George
Is woven into the tree's departure.
The way he used to limp
Through Henham Woods
As the rain slowly seeped
Through his battered raincoat.
His half bald head
Covered in a film of water
That shimmered in the sun
Like an over glazed pot.*

*And his worn shoes
Were the cut-off roots of the stricken tree
Wedging him firmly
To the living earth.*"

Matthew Booley 12 years.

Here, the child, through the power of language, has affirmed his own life source and something of his responsibility to this Earth.

Obviously, it is through our senses that we explore and discover the environment. Not only are our senses the means by which we grow to know our world and develop an aesthetic awareness; they are so often the means by which we remember. A fleeting smell, an evocative sound restores to us a time and a place. This sensuous experience is particularly authentic as the basis for writing when it comes through a literary connection made within a text. Seamus Heaney's poem "*Personal Helicon*", for example, restores to us our childhood fascination with water through the minutiae of his own sensuous memories:

"*the smells
Of waterweed, fungus and dank moss ...
I savoured the rich crash when a bucket
Plummeted down at the end of a rope.*"

Throughout the poem run echoes and reflections:

"*And one (well)
Was scaresome for there, out of ferns and tall
Foxgloves, a rat slapped across my reflection.*"

There is fearfulness here - and fear of the environment, when expressed in, and structured by, language, may well be a necessary prerequisite to the acceptance and appreciation which is finally resolved in a sense of responsibility. Unexpressed, unstructured, unresolved, it may well erupt into aggression and vandalism. So often vandalism is dubbed "mindless". It is the property of language to make us mindful of our world in all its beauty and all its fearfulness. The playful experimentation with reflection which Seamus Heaney describes is an underlining of the sensuous, often fearful, fusion between human beings and their environment; this is also an affirmation of their interdependence. The quest for knowledge of the world and our own place in it is a dangerous quest, no less dangerous when the childish play is over and:

*"I rhyme*
*To see myself, to set the darkness echoing."*

If children are to develop an aesthetic awareness of their world, they must dare to set their own darkness echoing.

Often it is local issues which release this impulse. In Suffolk, for example, a particularly contentious issue is stubble burning. I believe the following extracts from poems written on this theme demonstrate children making startling connections through their own sensuous impressions of a local area. Their writing is in itself a statement of the issue; while not a resolution of the problem it is, at least, a perception of the way in which man changes his environment simply in the pursuit of his daily work. So often, environmental issues are matters for delicate compromise, rather than clear cut issues of right and wrong. Within these extracts are subtle apprehensions of the beauty of the burning fields, strangely at odds with the despoliation and pollution of the landscape:

It is within literature that truth is expressed most finely and so often it is within the pages of a novel that a sense of place is inculcated. Within novels are landscapes more real than the actual places. Thomas Hardy's Egdon Heath, for example, is much more than a setting for his novel; it is a protagonist within it. Much has been written about the "personality" of this place. It is not a backdrop for the ensuing tragedy; much more a catalyst. The elements are likewise humanised:

*"Then Egdon was aroused to reciprocity; for the storm was its lover, and the wind was its friend."*

---

From "*Dancing Butterflies*"

*"Fields burn like rabbits*
                              *moulting.*
*The black ash floats*
*And drifts with the wind.*
*My hand feels the polluted air*
*But all it feels are the rare black*
                              *butterflies tickling"*
Gregory Block 13 years

---

From "*My Field*"

*"Then, a short life fails and*
                    *they die back down.*
*Fish of flame die on the black*
*water,*
*Eating at the golden left*
                              *overs,*
*And the red crabs move past*
*Slowly,*
*Black,*
*Creeping, stalking,*
*Soaking into the golden*
                              *brown."*
Lara Mair 10 years

---

And, moreover, it was:

*"perfectly accordant with man's nature - neither ghastly, hateful, nor ugly; neither commonplace, unmeaning, nor tame; but like man, slighted and enduring ... It had a lonely face, suggesting tragical possibilities."*

Further:

*"Civilisation was its enemy."*

It is, however, only the presence of human feeling which can invest a landscape with such "personality". The pathetic fallacy is surely one of literature's most compelling conventions - never a taming of the wilderness, rather a harnessing of the elements to the resolution of human conflict and a means by which we may indulge those atavistic yearnings Ted Hughes speaks of in "*Poetry in the making*":

*"These (beauty spots) are the remains of what the world was once like all over. They carry us back to the surroundings our ancestors once lived in for 150 million years."*

It is through the agency of places like Egdon Heath in novels like "*The Return of the Native*" that we are enabled to go home and renew these links with this wilderness earth our ancestors knew. We must make these places accessible to our children through the books they read. Only then can they know their beginnings and aspire to maturity.

When children meet places within the context of story, they cannot fail to deepen their apprehensions of their own landscapes. They begin to "know" them in the truest sense - the poetic sense. Within the world of children's literature there are books so enduring that as adults we feel we have always known them. "The Wind in the Willows" has such a place within our literary heritage. The world of the river bank is an enduring memory, not in the least blunted by the comfortable anthropomorphism. Always within the security of river bank and meadow lurks the menace of the Wild Wood - the wilderness that must inevitably be challenged. There are times when, like Mole, we do not want:

*"the warm clover and the play of seeding grasses"*;

we want the Wild Wood:

*"low and threatening, like a black reef in some*
                              *still southern sea."*

We must, like Badger, stake our claim there, and, at the same time, deepen our understanding of our interdependence.

And, of course, the episode of "*The Piper at the Gates of Dawn*", mystical and mysterious, must be read again and again, until its very familiarity has asserted and confirmed the Truth it embodies. At least there will be a dawning awareness of our World as a fearful and beautiful place which its inhabitants would do well to respect.

In citing one or two examples of place made important and accessible in literature, there is an overwhelming sense of all that has been left out. There are so many Egdon Heaths and Wild Woods in our literary heritage; teachers must make at least some of them available if children are to develop a sense of their own active role in the order of things on Earth.

Myth and fable are among the most powerful means by which lessons are learned. This is because they are not didactic; they operate at the level of story. Truth imparted through parable is inculcated at the deepest level where there is no need for explanation. The myth is the explanation and is entirely satisfying in itself. The myth of Persephone and the six pomegranate seeds is, again, one of those stories we feel we have always known. In the classroom it can be much more than a delightful explanation of the seasons. There is a great deal to be said for creative re-telling of a myth of this kind, provided that a new perspective is supplied, the essential excitement harnessed and structured by the exercise. Dreams can supply the necessary shift of perspective because they can contain the idea of selection. For instance, this exercise - imagine you are Persephone trapped in the cold darkness of the underworld. You fall asleep and dream of the good Earth from which you have been exiled. Recount your dream as you re-live the sights, sounds, textures, smells, tastes of your home - this is to direct attention to the minutiae of our environment while at the same time the role play involved provides the essential distancing of the conscious artist. Moreeover, within the context of Greek myth there is the sense of importance necessary to the creative act. From here there is a short step to writing a myth of our own time: imagine you are an astronaut exiled in Space within the clinical austerity of your space craft. Your senses crave the Earth you have left behind. Write a piece called: "*The Earthsick Astronaut*". Again, the onus is on the child to remember, in a moment of intense absorption, those aspects of Earth he appreciates most. The perspective provided precludes sentimentality and assists detachment. I believe the poem quoted here is both a celebration of the Earth which is the writer's home and also a means by which she was educated into a new appreciation of her immediate environment.

Then there are the great Creation myths of our various cultures. These attempts to explain and identify our sources are essential to the development of aesthetic awareness within the individual and also to the corporate well-being of mankind. We must know our own Creation story and read alongside it other great Creation myths like the Indian "Shatarupa". All this is to define our sources in a way which complements scientific discovery and, in doing so, confers a special dignity on man and the energy and curiosity with which he seeks the Truth within multifarious disciplines. For it is within literature that the false dichotomy between Science and the Arts is exploded. In particular, myth and poetry have this special function whereby literature does not just fill in the gaps left by scientists; it heightens and dignifies their quest for knowledge. Richard Church, in his autobiography "Over the Bridge", describes two occasions when he grew as human being and apprentice writer

---

"*The Earthsick Astronaut*"

"*He is yearning for his earth senses.*
*He wants the smell of burning wood to swirl up*
*And tickle his nose*
*Like a coarse, rough feather from a bird on the earth;*
*He wants the sight of a fire,*
*The flickering fish tails*
*That make his eyes see nothing else;*
*He wants to taste bacon, the real bacon,*
*Tingling on his tongue to evoke*
*The smell, the sound, the flavour..*
*He wants the touch of cold air on his skin;*
*Air, a free spirit, teasing, running;*
*A brush-past kiss on a warm cheek is*
*His memory;*
*And then ... the sad things;*
*Gravestones like babies' teeth, yet*
*Decayed with lichen and moss.*
*But still he is yearning,*
*Yearning for air, for fire,*
*For Earth.*"

Leonora Dack 12 years.

---

because he realised the "Oneness" of things. This was first the fusion which must take place between the Word and the Thing if integration is to take place. Secondly, it was an acknowledgment of the relationship between the Arts and the Sciences. Both experiences were literary and both transcended his personal antipathy to the reasoning world of the scientist. First, in the classroom, he stumbled across the words:

"*In the beginning was the Word, and the Word was with God, and the Word was God.*"

He writes:

"*I saw a new skyline defined. It was a landscape in which objects and words were fused. All was one, with the word as the verbal reality brought to material life by Mind, by man. It was therefore the very obvious, tangible presence of the Creator.*"

Then later, when struggling through an arid waste of quadratic equations:

"*I looked out through the grille of equations, and saw the old tree metamorphosed into a fountain of shuddering gold lights and green shadows. At the back of my mind was the inkling that somewhere, somehow, this play of sunshine, this lift and relapse of leaves, was a part of the same conjunction as I was expected to make in the solving of these equations in algebra.*"

Frustrated by the inadequacy of his reasoning brain, he turns to "*The Tempest*" where within:

"*the shape of its verse, its cadence, its opulent flood of vowels and the meaning it carried*",

42

he receives intuitively a "dreadful visitation". This is no denigration of the mathematician's quest for Truth, rather a firm statement of the Oneness of things. The disparate elements contained within this Oneness are, however, reconciled through the power of language. As Iris Murdoch says in "*The Sovereignty of Good*":

> "*There is only one culture, of which science, so interesting and so dangerous, is now an important part. But the most essential and fundamental aspect of culture is the study of literature, since this is an education in how to picture and understand human situations.*"

Children's attempts at their own Creation myths may seem, within these contexts, both stumbling and audacious. Nevertheless, they can be meaningful stages on the road to literacy and, at the same time, an assertion of the individual's role in the great history of mankind.

Fable equally has an essential role in environmental education. Ursula le Guin's "*A Wizard of Earthsea*" is both a parable of language and of conservation. It is no accident that these two issues are contained so compatibly within the same parable. In her essay "*Dreams Must Explain Themselves*" Ursula le Guin says her novel is:

> "*in one aspect about the artist ... the artist as magician. The Trickster, Prospero ... Wizardry is artistry. The novel is then in this sense about art, the creative experience, the creative process.*"

And linked with the creative process, and an essential part of it, is learning to know our world in the poetic sense. Apprentice wizards must learn the names of plants because:

> "*Magic consists in this, the true naming of a thing.*"

And:

> "*A magi can control only what is near him, what he can name exactly and wholly.*"

One young apprentice who naively asks the use of the plant fourfoil is told:

> "*When you know the fourfoil in all its seasons root and leaf and flower, by sight and scent and seed, then you may learn its true name, knowing its being which is more than its use.*"

This is both an articulation of the art of the poet and an affirmation of his necessary relationship with the world around him. In this sense we are all poets. We must all aspire to the mastery of language by which we:

> "*know by sight and scent and seed.*"

This is literacy. And it is linked inextricably with our relationship with Earth.

More than this, the novel explores the responsibility with which the wizard must exercise his power.

Where there is magic, there must be rules. There is, for instance, the matter of equilibrium. The world is held in delicate balance and power must be exercised with wisdom and caution. A young apprentice who longs to change a rock into a diamond has to learn that this would be to shake the balance of the world. There would be consequences. The needs of the world must always transcend the gratification of his own desires. Although all this underlines the special responsibilities of scientists today to maintain the balance of the world and conserve our resources with wisdom and prudence, there is no heavily didactic purpose within "*A Wizard of Earthsea*". Children read it at the level of exciting story and thereby are educated most effectively into their responsibility for this earth's resources.

And so, as English teachers, we may not teach environmental awareness; rather, through the special agency of poetry, story, myth and fable, we must inculcate it at the deepest level. We must have the courage to let the Word work within the carefully structured framework of a discipline which must take everything on trust and yet leave nothing to chance.

© Jill Pirrie, March 1988

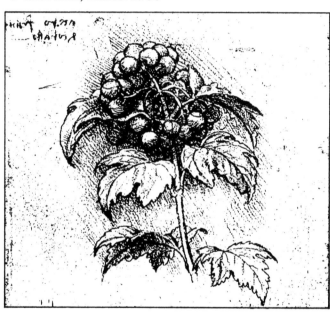

References

Church R. *'Over the Bridge'* Heinemann 1955

Grahame K *'The Wind in the Willows'* Methuen 1971

Hardy T. *The Return of the Native'* MacMillan 1954

Hart-Smith W. *'I Took My Mind a Walk'* Penguin English Stage One 1971

Heaney S. *'Selected Poems 1965-75'* Faber 1977

Hughes T. *'Wodwo Faber'* 1967

Hughes, T. *'Poetry in the Making'* Faber 1967

Le Guin U. *'Dreams Must Explain Themselves'* Agol. Reprinted in Signal 19 1976

Murdoch I. *The Sovereignty of Good'* Routledge and Keegan Paul 1970

Rogers T. *Those First Affections'* Routledge and Keegan Paul 1979

Tardios G. *The Way to Write'* John Fairfax and John Moat Elm Tree Books Hamish Hamilton 1981

# Environmental education and geography

Photograph: Sue Cunningham, Survival International

Malcolm Renwick
Director of Geography
for the Young School Leaver (Avery Hill) Project

# Environmental education and geography

Many of the concerns of environmental education coincide closely with those of geography. Of prime importance to both are the interactions between people and the physical, built and biological environments. Central to both environmental education and geography is the desire to encourage an interest in the environment and to build up **knowledge and understanding** of the processes shaping it. This is demonstrated by the following group of aims of geographical education taken from the HMI discussion document "*Geography from 5 to 16*".

Geographical studies should help pupils to:

◊ develop a strong interest in their own surroundings and in the world as the home of mankind;
◊ appreciate the variety of physical and human conditions on the earth's surface;
◊ recognise some of the more important geographical patterns and relationships which are revealed in different types of landscape and in different human activities;
◊ understand some of the relationships between people and environments;
◊ understand what it means to live in one place rather than another;
◊ understand some of the more important physical and human processes which produce geographical pattern and variety and which bring about change.

Geography is thus largely concerned with helping students make sense of their surroundings; it helps them to gain a better appreciation and understanding of the variety of physical and human conditions on the earth's surface. It is particularly concerned with the character of places and the role of individuals and societies,

modifying, creating and interacting with environments. Whilst the most significant contributions are likely to be in the human and social area, the subject is also concerned with the understanding of natural environments and the physical processes which lead to environmental stability or change. Without an understanding of the processes operating in natural systems such as landforms, weather and climate, vegetation and soils, students will be unable to make sense of the relationships between people and environments.

> **"Most environmental problems have a spatial dimension and it is this which makes the geographical perspective so important."**

Geography, of course, is not unique as a subject in its attempts to build up awareness, knowledge and understanding of the world in which we live. It does have a particular role to play in its emphasis on the importance of place, space and scale in the organisation of human activities. Thus geographical studies should help pupils:

◊ to appreciate the importance of geographical location in human affairs and to understand how activities and places are linked by movements of people, materials and information and by complex economic, social, political and physical relationships;
◊ to construct a framework of knowledge and understanding of their home area, their own country and other parts of the world, which will enable them to place information within appropriate geographical contexts.

Most environmental problems have a spatial dimension and it is

this which makes the geographical perspective so important. In its concern for place, space and scale, a school geography course ensures that study of the environment takes place at a variety of levels (local, regional, national, continental and global) and in a variety of contexts. By the careful selection of examples, an understanding is built up, albeit from a particular perspective, of the patterns and forms, processes and relationships found within particular environments; the spatial interaction within and between these are explored. In this way it is hoped that students will become "sensitive to the richness and variety of the earth's diversity."

Geographical education, however, is not now seen merely in terms of knowledge and understanding as demonstrated by the fact that it should help pupils to:

◊ appreciate the significance of people's beliefs, attitudes and values to these relationships which have a geographical dimension.

This recognises that important topics in the subject have obvious social and political dimensions. They cannot be properly understood without taking into account the attitudes and values of those involved in making decisions about the management of environments and the use of terrestrial space. In this way school geography increasingly addresses itself to the moral response to environments which inevitably leads to judgements of what is right and wrong. It awakens **concern** and care for the quality of present and future environments, natural and people-made, local and global. One cannot encourage informed concern for the environment without making efforts to arouse **responses** to the experience of environments. The important of sensory experiences, emotional responses and the need to encourage the importance of form, texture colour, detail and patterns as a prerequisite of aesthetic development are all evident by the frequent inclusion in fieldwork of perception exercises and landscape evaluation. In this respect geography plays its part in the ethical purpose of environmental education. Hopefully the outcome of this response to, and concern for, the environment will be reflected in action - considerate behaviour, practical improvement work and positive participation in decision-making processes.

In this way geographical studies in school have an important part to play in the education of young people by making a significant contribution to their response to, understanding of, and concern for the environment. All three elements should be covered in the geography syllabus - from infant to upper secondary - although probably in different proportions. In the early years, responding to direct experience of the local environment is likely to predominate, but not to the total exclusion of understanding and concern. For older students the scale will be extended to include regional, national and global issues with greater emphasis placed upon understanding and concern. Geographical studies should also help young people to:

◊ develop a range of skills and competences necessary to carry out geographical enquiry and interpret geographical information.

To understand geography adequately and to engage in geographical activities requires the development of a wide range of environmentally related **skills and competences**. These include investigations (often in the field) aassociated with observation, collection, representation, analysis, interpretation and use of data, including maps and photographs. The student benefits in terms of efficiency and satisfaction from the ability to read a map, interpret the urban and rural scene, visualise other places, anticipate the weather etc. - all important elements in environmental competence. The subject also provides many opportunities for self-motivated learning. This may involve the acquisition, analysis and evaluation of information from first-hand evidence and secondary sources; it may involve students in the need to distinguish relevant and non-relevant information and to arrive at informed opinions. Not least important are the opportunities to develop social skills provided by class and fieldwork activities, simulations and role play.

It follows that if geography is to maximise its contribution to environmental education, the choice of **content** of the syllabus should reflect the need for:

**a)** a balanced development of knowledge and understanding about four important themes:

(i) people, populations and their activities;

(ii) resources and materials, their use and misuse;

(iii) places, landforms, the processes forming them and their use;

(iv) living things, ecosystems, their manipulation, modification and use;

**b)** a study of environments at a variety of scales - local to global;

**c)** a choice of themes and environments that:

(i) demonstrate environmentally important concepts, generalisations and laws;

(ii) give opportunities for involvement in making value judgements, dealing with issues and decision making;

(iii) allow for the progressive development of environmentally related skills.

---

◊ A new situation is experienced, explored.
◊ Questions are raised, issues identified.

↓

◊ Answers, ideas, hypotheses, theories are suggested drawn from their own experience.
◊ Decisions are made as to how answers could be verified, ideas tested.

↓

◊ Data/evidence is collected through fieldwork, experiment, research of secondary evidence, experts.
◊ Data/evidence is processed, mapped, graphed etc.
◊ Data/evidence is analysed.

↓

◊ Findings are interpreted and evaluated.
◊ Conclusions are drawn.
◊ Original ideas are re-examined and confirmed/rejected/modified.
◊ Solutions are suggested.

↓

◊ Pupils complete work with enhanced knowledge and understanding- and with improved old skills or acquired new ones

This is essentially an ecological approach to the subject which makes contemporary people/environment issues at various levels of scale the focus of course construction. A study of such issues involves not only a grasp of the mechanics of environmental processes, but also of one's own and other people's stances in relation to an issue, and the processes of negotiation and decision-making which may occur. This is the perspective adopted by the Geography 16 - 19 Project, but many other courses have shown that such an approach can be handled by students from the beginning of their formal geographical studies if they are presented at the appropriate level.

Geography will only play its full part in environmental education and achieve the aims and objectives outlined above if it adopts teaching/learning processes which recognise young people as active rather than passive participants. If the emphasis is placed on the problem-solving and enquiry-based method described below, pupils will be given adequate opportunities to carry out practical investigations, to explore and express ideas, to apply ideas and skills to new situations, to interpret, analyse and evaluate information, and to reflect their own and other people's attitudes and values.

The teacher 'manages' this learning situation - carefully balancing what pupils can find out and do for themselves against what they need to have their attention drawn to and providing opportunities for them to acquire any additional skills they may require. In addition suitably designed role-play games and simulations can help pupils examine environmental decision making and the attitudes and values which influence these.

This brief paper argues that geography in schools can make important contributions to environmental education. It has a vital role to play, either as a separate subject or in an interdisciplinary situation, in:

a) influencing the choice of issue or problem;
b) emphasising spatial considerations;
c) seeking to establish as exactly as possible the inter-relationships of societies and environments;
d) employing as profitably as it can the full range of geographical concepts and skills.

By doing so we should achieve the fullest understanding of the environments people create and of the links behind those environments to the natural world. We may also ensure that the environments of tomorrow will be better than those of today.

©Malcolm Renwick, March 1988

### References
Beddis, R. A.'*Environmental Education: Core Curriculum or fringe activity?*' Bulletin of Environmental Education. July 1977.
DES '*The Environment - sources of information for teachers.*' 1979.
Haggett, P. '*Geography: a Modern Synthesis.*' Harper and Row. 1979.
Hall, D.'*Geography and the Geography Teacher.*' Allen and Unwin. 1976.
Hall, D.'*Knowledge in the Geography Classroom*' in 'The Geography Teachers' Guide to the Classroom' ed. Fien J., Gerber R., Wilson P.. MacMillan. 1984.
HMI '*Geography from 5 - 16*'. Her Majesty's Stationery Office. 1986.
Schools Council '*Main elements of the Curriculum Framework*'. Geography Curriculum Project 16 - 19. 1980.

# An historical perspective on environmental education

Photograph: Jordan Hill College

Dr Sneh Shah
Senior Lecturer
School of Education, Hatfield Polythechnic

# An historical perspective on environmental education

Environmental education focuses on an understanding of human and environmental issues. It analyses the nature, causes and consequences of the current environmental issues, and is concerned with the stimuli and structures that motivate and direct human behaviour towards the environment. It also aims at fostering an attitude of care and responsibility to the environment, illustrating the involvement of individuals, organisations and countries in the environment, and changes within it.

History has an integral part to play in such environmental education. The discipline is the study of human behaviour in the past. As such, it helps to explain why people behaved in the particular way that they did, in a variety of situations, at different times, and in different places. It is concerned with change, its complex nature, its causes, as well as continuity. It also helps to explain why different people have reacted to given factors in different ways, in different spatial and time contexts. In any analysis of human behaviour, environmental factors are likely to have had some influence, directly or indirectly.

Children in secondary schools need to learn how to relate to the world they are growing up in. The learning should also relate to their own lives and to their future responsibility as adults to make decisions.

History teaching focuses on children's insight into contemporary issues. One of the vital areas of current concern is the environment. Children should have enough understanding about the global, national and local issues to be able to make measured judgements as appropriate. History has a key role to play in providing the children with adequate KNOW-LEDGE and UNDERSTANDING of the background to the issues; ATTITUDES of care and responsibility to the environment within the context of the enriching relationships human beings can have with their environment; SKILLS to enable them to make reasoned judgements.

Historical narrative is concerned with explaining an event by tracing its intrinsic relations with other factors and events and establishing its historical context. For environmental issues this covers a very long time span, beginning with the state of the environment before human beings began to make an impact on it. The current condition of the environment is not something that has suddenly manifested itself, but something that has been caused by a series of occurrences over a long period of time. History can make an important contribution to children's understanding of the CONCEPT OF TIME. Giving the historical context of current environmental issues will enable children to appreciate how long it takes nature, for instance, to turn wood into coal and, similarly, how quickly it can be used up by human beings.

Knowledge and understanding of issues means more than a factual account; an analysis of the interaction of different factors shows how complex the background, as well as the solution, are. Establishing causation, an essential feature of history, necessarily means an understanding of political, social, economic and human factors. An understanding of the stimuli provides greater insights into the root causes of environmental problems. People need to become aware of the magnitude of the changes necessary when the root causes are complex.

In addition, the vast repertoire of experiences provided by history widens the range of relevant situations and factors. The exemplars can be located in different countries and at different periods. This range of experiences shows there is no inevitability about the nature, causes and consequences of environmental issues that human beings can relate to and adapt to their own environment in ways ranging from hostility to respect and care. An understanding of current issues involves an essential study of situations of CONTRAST.

Side-by-side a factual analysis and historical narrative where the children could be passive learners is a teaching approach that aims at EMPATHY. Asking the question why, trying to ascertain why people made the particular decisions at the particular time and place, is the beginning of the process of understanding the nature of the particular event. The children can establish different frames of reference.

At the same time, it is artificial to make a total distinction between the past and the present. The past is very much a part of the present. We are not necessarily individuals thinking independently about the past. Our way of life, values, beliefs and behaviour have been shaped in institutions and ideas which are themselves based on the past, the way the past has been interpreted and incorporated into current thinking and ingrained within a social system. We see the world in terms of our picture of it, which has been affected by the past. An attitude today of lack of care for the past could mean other issues were highlighted.

One way of understanding this is to apppreciate how the nature of history itself has changed. After the initial emphasis on political history, mainly of great individuals and events, economic factors began to loom large, particularly with the acceleration of industrial changes in Britain after the eighteenth century. Similarly, with the marked changes in population distribution and living conditions principally as a result of the industrial changes, social history began to be recognised as a legitimate part of history. Advances in archaeology have extended the scope of historical study. With the current focus on environmental issues, historians are already beginning to expand the acknowledged scope of the subject; the making of the English landscape is an example. Thus, as a study of human behaviour, history has to be seen to be a flexible discipline.

Similarly, the study of history does not just focus on content: as a method of inquiry, it involves the children in the experience of the process of historical thought. This includes locating, comprehending, interpreting and evaluating the different types of historical sources, ranging from documents to flora and fauna; making inferences from evidence available; and organising and presenting ideas on a reasoned basis. These skills are important in themselves, regardless of the context.

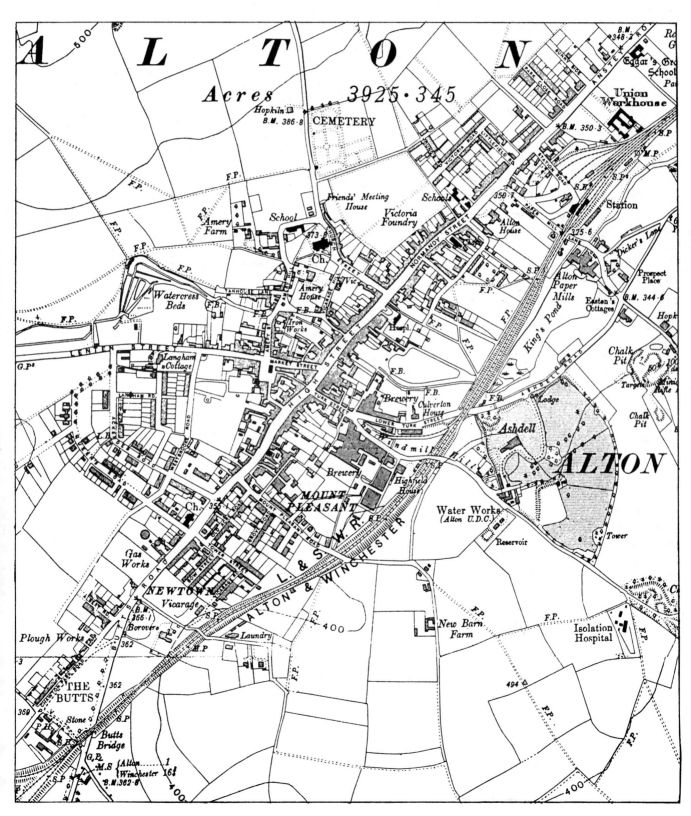

Thus the AIMS of history teaching with specific reference to environmental education are as follows:

**1.      Knowledge and understanding of:**
   a.    the early historical origins of current environmental issues;
   b.    the diverse responses of human beings to the natural environment;
   c.    the effects of technological changes on the natural environment;
   d.    the complex interplay of political, social, economic and other human factors on the environment;
   e.    the background to current global interdependence in economic and environmental issues;
   f.    the part played by individuals, organisations and countries in the decision-making process affecting the environnment;
   g.    the basis on which the importance of environmental issues is assessed in different times and places.

**2.      The development of attitudes that shall:**
   a.    increase children's inquisitiveness about their environment;
   b.    appreciate the aesthetic qualities of both the natural and human-made environments;
   c.    care about the quality of the environment;
   d.    appreciate how directly human beings can respond to their environment.

**3.      The development of skills to:**
   a.    appreciate the wide range of historical evidence; include those in the natural environment;
   b.    locate the evidence;
   c.    comprehend, interpret and evaluate the evidence;
   d.    organise and present the historical ideas on the basis of empathy and logic.

These aims can be fulfilled through the following content:

1.    WHAT IS HISTORY?
   An understanding of the process of historical thought is an essential part of the learning of history. The content and approaches in history teaching have a history of their own. Thus the main elements in this unit are:

   a.    The nature of historical evidence: this needs to include not only documents and artefacts but the totality of evidence that makes up historical sources. These include the archaeological sources; other clues in the landscape ranging from hedges and trees to river valleys; different forms of literary and other arts;
   b.    An analysis of such evidence in an historical study;
   c.    The selection of the relevant evidence and content based on what is perceived by individuals and societies at particular times as being important;
   d.    The interpretation of another generation's history and historical evidence.

2.    LOCAL STUDY (1)
   The value of the study of their own locality by the children is well established. The local study should ensure that:

   a.    its history is traced back as far as possible, highlighting the early natural environment;
   b.    an analysis of the evidence includes the environmental evidence;
   c.    an analysis of the evidence includes the changes in the natural and human-made environments, their causes and consequences;
   d.    a study of the evidence relating to the local environment includes relevant literary and artistic evidence;
   e.    the historical narrative includes issues of environmental importance and their significance;
   f.    the teaching approaches include participation by the children, especially in problem-solving exercises related to specific historical or contemporary events.

3.    LOCAL STUDY (2)
   By way of contrast, the children should study another locality which is very diverse in terms of natural environment and/or the changes to the locality as a result of human activity.

4.    NATIONAL STUDIES

Apart from the need to emphasize the human response to the environment in national studies, a common topic, the Industrial Revolution, should be expanded with the following as key elements:

a.    the British landscape before the major industrial changes beginning in the eighteenth century;
b.    an analysis of different factors, including human attitudes to the natural environment, that contributed to the major agricultural and industrial changes;
c.    the rate of formation of essential commodities such as coal and the rate of consumption;
d.    the consequences of the changes for the countryside;
e.    the consequences of the changes for the urban areas;
f.    the effect of the industrial changes in Britain on other countries such as India and China;
g.    action to restore some of the lost countryside, such as the beginning of the Garden cities.

5.    GLOBAL STUDIES

The World as One:

a.    case study of two geographically distant areas in the twelfth to the fourteenth centuries to illustrate diverse adaptations to the environment, and limited contact, if any, between the two areas;
b.    the historical background to the scientific, technical, economic changes leading to the contemporary interdependent world;
c.    the historical background to the consequent changes in economic and environmental issues and a detailed analysis of specific issues;
d.    the historical background to international organisations as an integral part of the "shrinking of the world"; detailed analysis of specific political, social/cultural, economic and environmental organisations.

6.    THEMES

The richness of the past can be experienced through the exploration of themes. The themes would illustrate the notions of change and continuity, and distinguish similarities and differences in different times and different places. Examples of themes are:

a.    Travel and exploration within the context of motives; the attitudes of the travellers and the people contacted to one another; the consequences for both;
b.    Trade and commodities within the context of motives; the cultivation and exchange of the specific commodities; and political, economic, environmental, social consequences of the trade for the producing and the buying people.

A range of topics such as these fit into the framework established by the overall aims. They also contribute to the children's understanding of the past, as they encompass studies ranging over a long time span, studies in depth and relating to the children's immediate experiences in the locality to the wider world at the national and international levels.

The METHODOLOGY adopted in the teaching of these topics should see the pupils not as passive learners but as active participants, contributing to their future role as decision-makers in the adult world. In order that the children may relate to history, which is by its definition likely to be distant from them, problem-solving exercises and role-play should be integral features.

The links between the past and the present are real but complex; the links between the past and the future are not clear-cut, as the axiom 'the past repeats itself suggests. However, young people can learn much from the past that will enable them to be responsible decision makers in the future. The past was what we had and while human beings will always want to bring about change, there is no inevitability about the nature of change. People create history and people can thus play an important part in defining the future which encompasses environmentally sound modes of living.

© Sneh Shah, March 1988

# Environmental education and technology

Photograph: Helen Tann

Brian Woolnough
Lecturer in Education(Science)
Department of Educational Studies University of Oxford

# Environmental education and technology

## 1. Introduction

Though there are many different perceptions about the meaning and definition of technology in school, about one thing there is full agreement. At the heart of technology lies a concern for the environment; at the centre of the technological process lies the determination to modify and control aspects of the world around us to the benefit of those living in it. Technology, arguably more than any other area of experience in the school curriculum, is committed to helping pupils to become responsibly aware of their environment and what they can do to care for and improve it.

The early definitions of technology by the Project Technology focused on this human purpose. *Technology is the purposeful use of man's knowledge of materials, sources of energy and natural phenomena (1968),* and *Technology is a disciplined process of using scientific, material and human resources to achieve human purposes (1970),* and this has been echoed in the GCSE National Criteria that the DES produced for the CDT: Technology courses (1985). This stated quite explicitly, as the seventh of its eight educational aims, the necessity:
*to encourage technological awareness; to foster attitudes of co-operation and social responsibility; to develop abilities to enhance the quality of the environment.*
It defined Technology as:
*principally concerned with design and problem-solving processes leading to the making and evaluation of artefacts and systems. It draws upon scientific principles. Technology also involves management of the environment and familiarity with the concepts of materials, energy and control.*

Perhaps the clearest and most helpful advocation of such a broad, environmental perception of the education to which all pupils are entitled was given by HMI in their discussion paper 'The Curriculum from 5 to 16 (1985)'. In the section describing the tech-

> "Technology, arguably more than any other area of experience in the school curriculum, is committed to helping pupils to become responsibly aware of their environment"

nological area of experience and learning, which all pupils should experience, it stressed:
*The essence of technology lies in the process of bringing about change or exercising control over the environment. This process is a particular form of problem solving: of designing in order to effect control. It is common to all technologies including those concerned with the provision of shelter, food, clothing, methods of maintaining health or communicating with others, and also with the so-called high technologies of electronics, biotechnology and fuel extraction and the alternative technologies of the Third World ...That (technological) content broadly concerns the nature and characteristics of natural and manufactured materials, and the nature, control and transformations of energy.*

So, clearly, the assertion that technology should be concerned with promoting environmental education is uncontentious. The fact that the DES through their proposals for a National Curriculum (DES 1987) includes Technology as a foundation subject for all pupils up to the age of 16 reaffirms the vital importance of this part of the curriculum.

## 2. Current realities for school technology

In practice, however, the happy agreement suggested above stops at the school gates, for there is no consensus yet as to the nature of school technology nor, indeed, for the reasons for teaching it. Different traditions in the school and different perceptions of the nature of technology have lead to four main approaches to the teaching of school technology, each with their own strengths, each having opportunity to develop environmental education, but each also with limitations and the possibility of missing out on this aspect in the subject. The four main approaches to technology I would label CDT, Hi-tec, Scientist and Integrationalist.

The CDT approach has developed from the craft areas of the school, with their traditions of making artefacts from wood and metal and their stress on craftmanship. Such departments have developed and widened their approach to include the design process in becoming Craft, Design and Technology (CDT). They stress the 'design, make and evaluate' process and necessarily include environmental considerations among the constraints and resources of the design brief. Whether such projects involve making a bird scarer, an office chair or a child's toy for the local play group, pupils should become increasingly aware of their environment.

The Hi-tec approach concentrates on giving pupils familiarity and competence in handling and using modern, high technology equipment in such areas as electronics, pneumatics, computers and robotics. Such technological devices are part of our environment and pupils should acquire the confidence to be in control of rather than to be controlled by, them. Furthermore, by using such apparatus in design-and-make projects, whether it is making alarm systems for the elderly, labour-saving devices for the kitchen, or equipment for extending the

> "The significance as far as environmental education is concerned lies in the traditional tension between economic growth and environmental protection."

facilities, and thus the quality of life, of the disabled, pupils are again brought into contact with the wider environment and made more aware of the needs of the community.

The Scientist's approach has two main thrusts. First the content of the science lessons has been increasingly seen in its 'social, economic and environmental' context, with pupils being made aware of the applications and implications of science in society. The growth of various Science, Technology and Society (STS) courses, (as described in the paper on science teaching, p 22), has done much to make pupils aware of the environmental aspects of their work. The second thrust within science has come through the introduction of investigational practical work in the science courses. Such projects might include an investigation of river pollution, of the erosion of local buildings or a study of the insect life in the school grounds.

The fourth approach, the Integrationalist's, sees technology very much as a multi-disciplinary approach and endeavours to build up the pupils' technological capability through working together on extended technological tasks. Professors Black and Harrison (1985) have argued this case well,

as has Peter Dutton (1987) in his stress on Technology for All Across the Curriculum (TAAC). Such tasks, whether it be the development of a school-promotion package for new pupils, the devising of an anti-hypothermia kit for old people or a study of the possibilities of using peanuts as energy supplies for people in countries with food shortages, inevitably cause pupils to become aware of, and personally educated in, the wider aspects of their environment.

In outlining these approaches I have shown how each can be, and often is, extremely useful for developing environmental education. There are those, however, who have advocated that all of Technology can be taught through one of these approaches alone. Such a claim can seriously restrict and distort the breadth of technology in schools and can mean that aspects of environmental education may be lost. It is possible for the CDT approach to limit its environment to that of the workshop, and the Hi-tec approach becomes merely 'toys for the boys' with the equipment becoming an end in itself. It is possible for the Scientist's approach to limit the technological task to the constraints of the syllabus and apparatus available, and to confine the problem solving to an environment limited to the laboratory. Even the Integrationalist approach can, because of the logistical constraints of the school timetable, staffing and organisation, make the task limited and contrived. Technology through any one of these approaches will not automatically develop an appreciation of the wider environment. However, the potential is there.

## 3. Rationale for Technological Education

Having considered some different approaches to technology in schools, it will be helpful to consider the rationale for teaching technology in schools, and then to

consider those aspects which constitute a balanced technological education for all. The underlying rationale is important, for quite different expressions of technology will develop from it, reflecting often covert underlying value judgements. The fundamental question relates to whether technology should be taught for vocational or educational reasons. Should it be taught to develop vocational skills and to provide adequate industrial 'manpower', or should it be taught primarily to develop each pupil's personal potential, as part of the broad education to which every pupil is entitled. Hopefully such alternatives are not mutually exclusive, but it would be true to say that some, such as TVEI, give much more to the former rationale while others, such as HMI, give more emphasis to the latter. The significance as far as environmental education is concerned lies in the traditional tension between economic growth and environmental protection. A short term emphasis on technology as a means of increasing industrial efficiency and economic profit could pay scant, and highly selective, attention to the needs of the environment in the local, the national and the international context. I would advocate that all pupils should be taught technology as part of their broad, liberal education, through which they would develop an appreciation of their world and its culture, build up problem solving and decision making skills and gain a personal maturity which would enable them to play an active part in being in control of their environment. Such an educational approach in the encouragement of responsible, autonomous citizens, would also, I believe, be in the best long term interests of our world and provide an appropriate preparation for adult life and employment, both in industry and in the service and caring professions.

The technological education of each pupil should consist of four distinct but interrelated strands:

56

technological literacy, technological awareness, technological capability and information technology (IT). Some of these strands should be experienced through existing subjects and areas of study; others would necessitate a discrete time allocation in the curriculum. (N.B. the ordering of these strands is not significant; no sequential hierarchy is to be inferred.)

In Technological Literacy each pupil should be made familiar with the content and the methodologies of different technologies. There is a range of technologies, not just one, containing different knowledge and approaches, about which all pupils should know and understand. (As we are familar with talking about the arts, the humanities and sciences as plural, collective terms, so we should envisage the technologies.) It is not appropriate to seek to define absolutely, at this stage, the content of this strand of technological education; indeed it might well change with time and with the local context. However, it should include a broader range of technologies than those traditionally associated with mechanical and electrical engineering, and should also include those relating to the production and utilisation of textiles and food, to the provision of housing and health, and to both 'high technology' and alternative technologies. There already exist good exemplars for much of this in the existing curriculum of CDT, home economics, computer studies and science departments. More work needs to be done to produce a comprehensive, co-ordinated curriculum in this area, and to make much of the existing material less gender biased. For pupils to be technologically literate in modern society they should have a sound appreciation of these aspects of our culture.

For Technological Awareness, along with a knowledge of the different technologies, each pupil should be made aware of the personal, moral, social, ethical, economic and environmental implications of such technological developments. Such an awareness should be developed in the context of most subjects and areas of study: through history, geogaphy, and English as well as through the sciences, home economics, technology and CDT.

For Technological Capability, in addition to being knowledgeable about different technologies and aware of their implications on society, every pupil should be encouraged to develop their own technological capability in tackling a technological problem, both independently and in co-operative action with others. Such a capability would tackle realistic practical problems which require consideration from a variety of perspectives: technical, scientific, aesthetic, environmental, social and moral. It would utilise knowledge, both explicit and tacit, from a variety of disciplines and incorporate the use of the 'technological process' with all its inherent humanity of 'trial and error' based on personal experience and creativity, feedback and evaluation. This would involve active engagement with technological tasks and would require a significant amount of time to allow for an adequate response. These activities would be synthetic, bringing together knowledge, experiences, resources and skills acquired in other subject areas. As such, they would differ from the traditional subject-based approach adopted in many secondary schools, being more similar to the interdisciplinary, topic-based work of the primary schools. Though it is possible to develop technological capability in other subjects, notably CDT, home economics and science, it is likely that the most effective approach will necessitate a more interdisciplinary structure.

For Information Technology, each pupil should acquire competence and confidence in the technological handling of information during their school life, both as a preparation for life in modern society and also as an important skill required for developing technological capability. This should be taught as an integral part of different subjects or as appropriate to a particular task, rather than as a separate subject.

Permeating and overarching the technological education that pupils receive through these four strands in their formal curriculum, each pupil should receive their education in a school ethos which regularly encourages technological activities. This might include technological clubs, inventors, posters and 'great egg race' type competitions, fashion design shows, animal and horticultural clubs, displays of technological projects, school plays, young enterprise and CREST ventures, and activities in PSE. Such a technological ethos would do much to encourage a mature and sympathetic awareness of the local, as well as the wider, environment.

## 4. The Way Forward

Much of this paper has been spent clarifying the framework in which technology is taught, with examples given to illustrate each aspect. This, I believe, has been necessary, for until some coherent

> "There is already much good work in each of the different approaches to teaching technology which is central to environmental education."

rationale is agreed for technology in schools there will be no constructive development which will encompass all the important aspects. Furthermore, school need to develop whole schoo policies for technological an environmental education to ensu they are covered sensibly, adequate ly and in a co-ordinated manner.

There is already much goo

work in each of the different approaches to teaching technology which is central to environmental education. The national criteria for the GCSE examinations and the expansion of the HMI views of the areas of experience and learning, to which all pupils are entitled, have provided a good basis for this. Now we look to the Technology Working Group for the National Curriculum to ensure that the broadest interpretation of technology will be developed as suggested above. Following those guidelines, with the emphasis on design at the heart of technological capability, and a comprehensive and liberal development of the curriculum for technological awareness and literacy, pupils will be helped to develop into mature, responsible, self-confident citizens, well aware of their responsibilities and potential for helping to

control their environment, motivated and able to make their world a better place.

There is, however, an alternative path that could be followed. Technology in schools could be perceived in utilitarian, mechanistic terms, aimed at providing for the short term needs of a materialistic, self-centred, aggrandizing society. The subject could be taught as a means of providing for the skills needed for modern western industry to increase its economic prosperity, without due regard to the social, personal and moral implications of such technology in the local and worldwide environment. Technology without compassion and humanity would become dangerous, indeed fatal. Technology without skills could be ineffective. Our challenge is to ensure that the teaching of technology in schools encourages the

personal, moral and autonomous, attitudes for responsible citizenship in the future as well as developing the skills which will enable that compassion to be turned to good effect.

© Brian Woolnough, March 1988

**References:**

Black, P. and Harrison, G.B. *In Place of Confusion.* Nuffield- Chelsea Curriculum Trust, London 1985

D.E.S. *The National Curriculum 5 - 16,* a consultative document. H.M.S.O., London 1987

Dutton, P. *Technology for All Across the Curriculum,* M.S.C., Sheffield 1987

H.M.I. *The Curriculum from 5 to 16.* H.M.S.O., London 1985

Secondary Education Council. (1985) *National Criteria for C.D.T.* S.E.C., London